ALAN L. H

THE GENDER REVOLUTION

Emancipating Women and
Empowering the Church

RIVER
PUBLISHING

River Publishing & Media Ltd
Bradbourne Stables
East Malling
Kent
ME19 6DZ
United Kingdom

info@river-publishing.co.uk

ISBN 978-1-908393-59-3
Cover design by www.spiffingcovers.com
Printed in the United Kingdom

CONTENTS

WHAT OTHERS ARE SAYING...

"Alan's excellent book is both well written and much needed. For too long the Church, generally speaking, has been neglectful in its understanding of the importance and significance of seeing women recognised and then fully released into all aspects of Christian ministry, including 'leadership'.

From a deep conviction brought about by both a deep study of the Scriptures and years of pastoral ministry, this biblical yet practical overview of the subject is a 'must read' for all, and I thoroughly recommend it."
John Partington National Leader Assemblies of God G.B.

"The book you hold in your hand not only contains a considered and sound theological contribution to a crucial arena within the Church, it also represents a journey of revelation, humility, obedience and transformation for the author. In the pages that follow you will hear reason and feel passion, as the author returns us to the God-image in women, restoring them to their rightful place, beside men!"
Dr John Andrews, Principal of Mattersey Hall

"Alan Hewitt has been teaching the Bible for over 40 years and is a well-respected and gifted pastor, leader, communicator and teacher. In this book he challenges the way the Church has mishandled and misrepresented the teachings of the Bible on a massively important issue – that of the ministry of women in the Church of Jesus. This book will challenge, confront and hopefully convict the reader, to revisit and rethink what the Bible really teaches about this vitally important issue. This book is a well thought out and passionate plea for God's Church to allow Jesus to have all and not just some of His gifted people in the 21st

Century Church at His disposal, so that they can serve, stand and speak for Him without restriction in every setting He requires!"
Grayson Jones (MA in Missional leadership)

"I did not commence my ministry 46 years ago supporting the leadership role of women in ministry. When, however, I realised that the women who were denied leadership positions in the West were supported by the same people who had restricted them, if they wanted to go to the most dangerous parts of the world to work as missionaries, it seemed to me that the situation was clearly incongruous and needed further examination. If the 21st Century Church is to fulfil its mandate, then the whole Church, men and women alike, must embrace the whole task wholeheartedly. This timely book encourages us to do just that."
Rev John Glass, General Superintendent Elim Pentecostal Churches UK

"There are two things about this book that make it a MUST READ! Firstly, the author is a man who, through the pursuit of God and His Word, has never failed to allow God to lead his life. I have watched in wonder as Pastor Alan Hewitt has led church with radical faith, unwavering devotion and a conviction so deep that he stands as an example for younger pastors and leaders to follow. Secondly, the content is remarkable. *The Gender Revolution* was just that in Alan's life. Through studying the Word of God and having the depth of conviction to change his mind on cultural barriers, he has successfully led his church through this revolution. The man is remarkable; the content comes from this man's journey of faith! A must read! We are big fans of this man!"
Glyn & Sophia Barrett, !Audacious Church, Manchester, UK

"*The Gender Revolution* is not simply an argument affirming women in ministry; it's an invitation to join an experienced Bible

teacher in his own mind-changing journey of discovery."
Joel Edwards, Strategic Adviser, Christian Solidarity Worldwide (CSW)

"With each generation we see societies growing to accept women as leaders in their own right. However, there are two major reasons why women stop short of achieving God's purpose for their lives. Firstly, whether it's in the ministry or the marketplace, they lack an understanding of where God has positioned them. Secondly, they are unable to claim and/or act upon their God-given authority.

The Bible records the journeys of women who, despite societal norms and personal fears, stepped out in faith to live out God's purpose in their lives. I believe this book will help to reveal God's perspective on women in leadership, break long-held mind sets/perceptions, and enable women to step into places of purpose and leadership."
Rev Dominic Yeo, Senior Pastor of Trinity Christian Centre. General Superintendent of the Assemblies of God of Singapore; Chairman of the Asia Pacific Assemblies of God Fellowship; Advisory Council Member of the Pentecostal World Fellowship

DEDICATION

*To my mother – who spent her life loving God yet living in the
dark shadows of Patriarchy.*
*To my wife Jennifer – who had high expectations for me, even
though they weren't reciprocated.*
*To my two daughters – Rachel and Adele, whose lives have risen
above my blinkered stereotype.*
*To Hope Church Newtown – who bravely opened their hearts to
a fresh understanding of the Scriptures and took the leap from
tradition to truth.*
*To Denise, my Associate Pastor, an undeniable evidence that God
gives leadership gifts to women.*
*To all those women around the world who have been freed by
Christ, but shackled by their church.*
*And, supremely and above all, to Jesus Christ, who died to fully
redeem Eve as well as Adam.*

ACKNOWLEDGEMENTS

My sincere thanks to Kashmira Bhatt for her many hours of proofreading whilst also fulfilling a very responsible role lecturing at a local college. Kashmira, a single parent, has raised two amazing children who are both missionaries – her daughter in Asia and her son here in Newtown, Wales. Kashmira, I salute you!

I would also like to express my deep gratitude to Tim Pettingale of River Publishing for his encouragement, advice and editorial input which has made this book possible.

FOREWORD

This book is big, much bigger than it looks. It doesn't tower over you like *War and Peace* or some similarly huge tome. But make no mistake, this book is *big*.

At first glance you might think this is just about women. Of course, it is, but it's so much bigger than that. This is also a book about the Church. For far too long, far too many Christian communities, organisations and denominations have skirted around addressing their views on how our sisters in Christ can serve His Church. Some people have taken this seriously, others have dismissed it, but all the while the Church has been suffering because at least half, often more, of its members are being restricted, even resisted, in working out the call that God has placed upon them. In this book Alan unpacks for you why the Church is unnecessarily, and un-biblically, hindering and limiting itself by preserving a hierarchy of status between men and women.

Ultimately, however, this book is even bigger than that, because as Alan continues to unpick traditions, ideas and biases that he shows don't originate from Jesus, you will begin to realise that this is actually a book about the Gospel. If God really has brought us all together as one in Christ Jesus, as Paul argues in Galatians 3:26-29 (make sure you read the excellent Magna Carta chapter on those verses), then the decision to exclude women from full incorporation into the life and leadership of the body of Christ threatens to overturn the liberating core of the Gospel.

As I said, this book is BIG.

Alan writes with an easy style and a sharp mind. As with all good Bible teachers, his simple sentences leave you pondering long after you've finished reading them. He writes with honesty and vulnerability, but also with a passion and compulsion that places the reader in no doubt as to how seriously committed he is to this subject and his desire for the Church to take it seriously too.

I love what Alan has accomplished with this book. I love it because I am convinced that if the Church is to run properly in the future that God has planned for it, then it needs to fix the limp that's being caused by a Gospel-resisting insistence that only its male members can lead. Paul's vision of the Church in Ephesians 3:10 is a multi-faceted representation of God's wisdom expressed by the "unity in diversity" that sets the Church in stark contrast to other organisations in the world, divided as they are by issues of distinction. One thing I am certain of is this: if the Church insists on maintaining separation and segregation on the basis of personal identity rather than a person's identity in Christ, it will have departed dangerously from the Gospel and Jesus' vision of the Kingdom of God. I hope this book will make you certain of this too.

Some of you will belong to church communities that are asking or imagining how to work out the beautiful vision of equality that is the Church of Jesus. In your world, Alan's book will be like a coach on the side lines of your race, encouraging you to keep going until you see this equality for real. For other church communities, the idea of women leaders in your church is *more than you can ever ask or imagine*" (Ephesians 3:20). If that is you, then Alan's book will be like a prophet proclaiming the possibilities of what God can do amongst you. Perhaps some readers will feel that Alan is wrong and you won't like what he has to say. I urge you to read his book anyway, engage with it, think about it, wrestle with it and argue with it. But let me warn you, bring you're "A game" because Alan doesn't pull his punches.

As you might well gather by now, I think this book is for you. Like Paul said of Phoebe, the female deacon, in Romans 16, "I commend Alan to you." This book will challenge you, but like all the best challenges it will also present you with an opportunity to change how you think and act. It's up to you whether you do or not. For the sake of our mothers, sisters and daughters in the Gospel, and for the Bride of Jesus that is his Church, I hope and pray that you do.

Grace and peace,

David S. Harvey

Lecturer in New Testament, Mattersey Hall, UK

27th January 2016 – Holocaust Memorial Day

INTRODUCTION: PATRIARCHY, COMPLEMENTARIANISM & EGALITARIANISM

Any study into the subject of gender in the Church will inevitably include some uncommon words.

There are broadly three ways of viewing the relationship between men and women. I prefer not to use the word "feminism" as I do not think it is helpful and can sometimes give people the wrong perspective, especially in the Church. (However, it is worth pointing out that the basic definition of "feminist" is simply someone who believes women are equal with men).

One view is known as "Patriarchy", which holds that leadership in the church, home and public life, is exclusively for men. This view, also known as "traditionalist" believes that different gender-roles were part of God's created order and that a woman's role is therefore to look after the home and be submissive to the man. The woman should submit to her husband in the home, to the male leaders of the church, and should not seek positions of leadership in society.

The next view, known as "Complementarianism", holds that men and women are equal but with different roles that complement each other. Ultimately, this usually has the same end result as Patriarchy in that women often are not allowed to occupy leadership positions.

The third view is known as "Egalitarianism". Though the word is quite a mouthful, I believe it conveys the true teaching of Scripture: that men and women were created totally equal and have joint and shared responsibility in marriage, society and ministry.

It is useful to know a little about these last two views.

During the 1980s evangelicals debated much about women's roles and although the views varied, two main camps polarised the main opinions. First in 1984 an "Evangelical Colloquium on Women and the Bible" was held in Oak Brook, Illinois, and this was followed in 1987 by a group calling themselves the "Council for Biblical Manhood and Womanhood". This group produced a statement posturing Complementarian views a year later in 1988. Their statement asserted that though Man and Woman were created equal, their roles were different and that there should be male headship in the church and the home. One of the major works from this school is a lengthy series of essays published in 1991 called, "Recovering Biblical Manhood and Womanhood", edited by John Piper and Wayne Grudem. This work has played a huge role in restraining women from ministry and leadership in the Church.

In response to this Complementarian surge another group rose up calling itself the "Christians for Biblical Equality", which represents the Egalitarian point of view and holds that on the basis of Galatians 3:28 and other biblical texts, that men and women are equal and should be free to operate in their God-given gifts.

During the last 30 years much has been written from both camps and the debate between Complementarians and Egalitarians basically comes down to four questions:

- Does the Bible teach a hierarchical structure of male and female relationships?
- Do we find women in leadership positions in the Bible?
- Do women in the Bible function in the same leadership roles as men?
- Does the Bible restrict women from certain leadership roles?

Naturally, my short summary of these two opposing views is quite simplistic, but I think the reader will get a clearer understanding of my egalitarian view as we proceed. Perhaps the best way to distinguish between the two is this: Complementarians want Christians to believe that women's *worth* is equal to men's. Egalitarians want Christians to believe women's *rights* are equal to men's.

Explaining the difference between these two views, Carolyn Custis James states:

"Egalitarians believe that leadership is not determined by gender, but by the gifting and calling of the Holy Spirit, and that God calls all believers to submit to one another."

The stance of Complementarians is different in that,

"...they believe the Bible establishes male authority over women, making male leadership the biblical standard."[1]

There is a huge difference between these two viewpoints, which is why I stand boldly in the Egalitarian camp. I have witnessed so many Christian women being told that they are equal, yet being treated as if they are not. I hope people of all sides will read this book and then make a fresh judgement about this vitally important matter.

Endnote:

1. Bessey, Sarah, *Jesus Feminist* (Howard Books, 2013) p15.

CHAPTER 1
CONFESSIONS
OF A MISOGYNIST

"Misogynist" is an infrequently used word, but one that describes many in our society. Sadly, I was one. It sounds as bad as it is. The word has its root in two Greek words and describes someone who, "views women as inferior to men ... a male chauvinist ... a person with a prejudice against women..." or even "hates women". Thankfully, I wasn't in the last category, but I did view women as people who basically were put on the planet to assist men in fulfilling their destiny. I know, that is sad. But I also know that I am not unique in having suffered from the dreadful disease of misogyny.

Having pastored two churches during the course of more than 45 years of Christian ministry, I am as shocked as anyone that I should write a book – especially on the subject of women in leadership. I was raised in a local church where women wore hats and knew their place. It was the men who "did" church, apart from on a Wednesday afternoon when there was the women's meeting and, of course, Sunday School. It was okay to trust the women with the children for an hour. I always wondered why there wasn't a specific men's meeting – but of course they had that each Sunday when the men led church, preached and served communion, while the women washed the glasses and ironed the white cloth that covered the table. There was an invisible protocol that everyone conformed to: if a married woman had a conviction about something or a strong personality, it was silently assumed that "she wears the trousers in that house!" A few women in our church were referred to as "Jezebel" whenever they wore make up or stepped out of line.

Life at home mirrored this patriarchal ethos. My father was the one who held the authority and my mother was the homemaker who did the washing, cooking, ironing and cleaning. Not once can I remember my father ever ironing or doing what was known as a "feminine job". To me, this was the right way and the two years I spent at Bible College only reinforced this stereotype, so that when I began pastoring a church in 1972, I followed the pattern and kept women "in their rightful place" – even teaching that women in unhappy and sometimes abusive marriages should submit to their husbands. I was not alone. There have been many examples where women have suffered abuse because men have quoted Scripture at them, insisting that their submission is God's will and a biblical principle.

Sensing a call to ministry from the age of 18, it was obvious to me that my future wife would also serve MY call. It never crossed my mind that a woman could have a call of her own, other than to raise a family and support her spouse. When it came to the preparation for MY ministry (even though by then we then had an 8-week old daughter), I moved my young family in with my parents so that I could be obedient to God's call on MY life. I remember going to Bible college and discovering that there were in fact women there too. With shame I admit that I showed them little respect and often asked them what they were planning to do when they left, because "women don't do ministry!"

Looking back now I see how biased and prejudiced I was. It wasn't simply a blind spot – more like a total blackout, especially when it was my wife who had to take on several jobs to provide for the family and help to pay MY fees!

As a young minister I attended the Assemblies of God annual conferences and looked with disdain on the few female pastors who were present, thinking of them as "usurpers of authority". Certainly out of place. The idea of women elders, deacons, preachers, trustees or leaders was out of the question in my local church, though a female missionary could tell a children's story or give their testimony! In the book, The Black Swan Effect, Felicity Dale refers to one lady missionary who said, "It would seem that there is an unwritten rule that goes like this: 'A woman must never, never, ever have spiritual authority over a man unless that man lives in a remote part of the world and has skin at least two shades darker than her own.'"[1] Ouch!

This was the pattern set for me that would continue during years of ministry. After 13 years of leading a wonderful church in north Manchester, in 1985 I moved with my family to Newtown in mid-Wales to lead what is now known as Hope Church, where I still function in the role of Senior Pastor. It was the type of church I'd been accustomed to – one in which the leaders, trustees and deacons were all men, and on a Sunday morning twelve men stood across the front in a long row to serve communion and take the collection. The idea of having women involved was not on the agenda for consideration.

It was in this beautiful area of Wales, and in this great church, where a huge paradigm shift in my world view would take place, challenging me to think again and to search the Scriptures more deeply than ever before. Uncomfortable though it was, it was here that I was compelled to recognise that there were women who were anointed by the Holy Spirit, who were not rebellious, and who were gifted with leadership ability – and I had the responsibility of either restraining them or releasing them into God's plans and purposes for their life. I had always encouraged men in this way, but had been blinded by gender prejudice on the basis of my tradition and an inadequate understanding of certain scriptures.

I recall being invited to preach at Spring Harvest, the largest Christian event in the UK, and after accepting the invitation, discovering that in certain streams I was to be paired to speak with female leaders. In retrospect, two things shocked me. One was the inner struggle I had to contend with in sharing the platform and the Word of God with a woman. The other was having to admit how good they were!

The crunch came for me with Denise, my youth pastor's wife. I had invited this married couple to join our team and pastor the youth with the expectation that the wife would be a blessing to the girls, but Denise showed that she had a much greater capacity than the role assigned to her. She had an insatiable appetite, passion and hunger for the local church, together with revelation, insight and high emotional intelligence. To me, the gift was right but the gender was wrong. As a consequence, I would train, encourage and empower young men to serve, developing our leadership team accordingly, while this gifted young woman remained at home. I recall her coming into my office one day and informing me that though she was full-time in youth work, she was under-utilised and suggested that maybe she should get a part-time job outside the church. I had a problem. One that I had struggled with for some time. It wasn't that I doubted her ability, just that she did not fit my theology. Some time after Simon, her husband, had received his ministerial credentials with the Assemblies of

God UK, Denise came to my office asking me if she could apply for credentials too. My instant response was, "Why? Simon has them! Why do you need them?"

This disconnect between my theological stance and the clear gift of God caused me to wrestle with the subject. I was compelled to read all I could on the subject and especially to study afresh those passages in the Bible that seemed to bar women from leadership in the church. I found this exercise very challenging. I love theology and the rich writings of the reformed tradition, and many Bible teachers I greatly admire seemed to support my prejudice with strong scriptural backing. However, the more I researched, the more I discovered that some of their arguments lacked true biblical integrity. There is always the danger that we interpret Scripture in line with our preferred, comfortable traditions. I was also aware that, for me personally, to change my views on women in leadership after practicing patriarchy for many years would make me vulnerable to criticism.

But the deeper I delved into Scripture, the more I was challenged and enlightened. One result of this is that today, the youth pastor's wife is now my Associate Pastor, her husband an Assistant Pastor, and we have other women on our leadership team. This has been revolutionary and an immense blessing in the life of our church.

Before I get into the full story of my journey to reach this point I need to state two things. Firstly, I am aware that the subject is still controversial amongst evangelicals and in no way do I want to disrespect fellow Christian leaders who hold a different view. Like them, I believe the Bible is the infallible Word of God and my position is not taken in spite of it, but because of it. But those who oppose women in leadership do not have a monopoly on the faithful handling and application of Scripture. Our understanding may differ and, as I myself once held a different view, I am fully aware of the strength of feeling this matter can evoke. I have even been called "a preacher of heresy", simply because I have taught the wonderful truth of an all-inclusive redemption for Eve as well as Adam.

Although feelings are strong and run deep on both sides of the argument I think it's worth reminding ourselves of a statement made at the Third Lausanne Congress on World Evangelization in Cape Town 2010:

> "We recognise that there are different views sincerely held by those who seek to be faithful and obedient to Scripture. Some interpret apostolic teaching to imply that women should not teach or preach, or that they may do so but not in sole authority over men. Others interpret the spiritual equality of women, the exercise of the edifying gift of prophecy by women in the New Testament Church, and their hosting of churches in their homes, as implying that the spiritual gifts of leading and teaching may be received and exercised in ministry by both women and men. We call upon those on different sides of the argument to accept one another without condemnation in relation to matters of dispute, for while we may disagree, we have no grounds for division, destructive speaking, or ungodly hostility towards one another."[2]

I think this is helpful, but easier said than done!

Secondly, this is an enormous subject and my book could easily have been two or three times its present size, but I have written this book with the "normal" Christian in mind and endeavoured to make it as readable as possible. For this reason I have kept the use of Hebrew and Greek words to a minimum, and references/citations are placed at the end of each chapter. It is my view that many Christians do not read books because they feel intimidated by scholarship, so I have attempted to write a book that people will read. Others have written wonderfully from an academic standpoint and I refer to their books in the "Recommended Reading" list with thanks to God for each of them. I hope that the reader of my book will have a hunger to study the subject in greater detail. I particularly recommend for the scholar the book, Man and Woman, One in Christ by Dr Philip Barnton Payne who wrote his 500 page treatise after over thirty years of textual study.

This book is simply written by a Pentecostal pastor who believes that the time has come for the Church in the 21st Century to honour, release and embrace all the God-given gifts in the Body of Christ, regardless of gender. Although the book is not intended to be academic, neither is it theologically naïve, and I trust that the reader will see that in order to release women fully into their God-given gifting, we do not need to compromise on the teaching of Scripture. In my view, the compromise of Scripture occurs when we do not release women.

My prayer is that this book will help both pastors and people to read the Bible in a fresh light, to encourage the many women who feel frustrated by limited opportunities, and to assure men that they do not lose masculinity when women called by God serve within their gifting. I will also maintain that women can remain feminine, yet fulfil every office or ministry referred to in the New Testament.

Without wanting to sound over-spiritual, I believe that the discussion around this subject at this time, of which this book is a part, is divinely commissioned. My prayer is that it will challenge centuries' old bias and prejudice in the Church. My heart is carrying a strong burden for this message, that I believe is not merely natural, but has a sense of mandate I cannot escape. I believe that the Lord wants to encourage and sponsor the greater releasing of women in the body of Christ to their full destiny in the purposes of God.

I hope that this simple book will be part of a much wider campaign that, thankfully, is already underway and by God's grace will lead to the freedom and emancipation of women in the Church of Jesus Christ. Many great books have been written on this subject, but not many by men. Sadly, for that reason, they have not been given the respect they deserve. I hope that the fact this book has been written by a pastor who has been forced to make a huge U-turn will win the subject wider attention. I have been encouraged in my task by many others who have done a similar U-turn. Dr Scott McKnight is one who has publicly apologised to his former college students. With humility he states simply, "We were wrong."[3] The distinguished New Testament scholar, R. T. France is another Bible teacher who has had fresh revelation on this issue and moved to an inclusive view of women's roles in ministry. In his book Women in the Church's Ministry, France makes a very significant point which notes that he has never met an evangelical who has changed their mind in the opposite direction. That is worth thinking about![4]

Let me state for the record that the goal of this book is not to bring men down, but to lift women up. Many are blinded to the truth that until women are fully free, men cannot be fully free either.

Endnotes:

1. Dale, Felicity, The Black Swan Effect, Kingdom Heart Publishing (2014) p237.
2. McKnight, Scott, The Blue Parakeet, Zondervan (2008) p150.
3. 3rd Lausanne Congress on World Evangelisation, Capetown, 16-125 Oct 2010.
4. France, R. T., Women in the Church's Ministry, Eugene, OR: Wipf & Stock (1995) p92.

CHAPTER 2
THE SHAMEFUL
ABUSE

The annals of the world's history carry a disgraceful record of the mistreatment and disrespect of women. Javier Moscoso in the book, *Pain, a Cultural History*, tells the story of Eufame Macalyne who was burned alive in 1591 for seeking pain relief when she gave birth to her two sons. The rationale behind the decision to burn this Scottish woman of rank was that God had cursed women with pain in childbirth, so she should accept it. To prevent pain would be a circumvention of His will.

Scottish physician and surgeon Sir James Simpson was also confronted with this view when, in 1847, he argued with the medical and theological community that God would not be opposed to his use of chloroform to anaesthetize women during childbirth as God Himself had used it when performing surgery on Adam in Genesis 2:21.[1]

There is no doubt that the female gender has paid the biggest price for the tragedy that happened in Eden. What makes it worse is that often Scripture has been used to justify their pain and suffering.

In April 1989, the magazine *Christianity Today* reported that a Lutheran pastor faced formal heresy charges because he had dared to even ask the church to consider whether its attitude to women and their role could be looked at. He said, "My aim is to strip away the sexism of the Church and get back to the root of how Jesus and the Apostles treated women. In my opinion, we are wearing cultural blinders. I want to ask the Church, do the beliefs we hold reflect the biblical message? And can we divorce ourselves from the centuries of conditioning, set our blinders aside for a minute and look at how our Lord considered the role of women."

It was for these questions that this pastor was summoned to his denominational headquarters to face the charge of heresy.

In 1988 Ann Graham Lotz, daughter of Billy Graham, was asked to speak at a pastors conference. When she stood up to address the audience some of the men there turned their chairs around to face the other way. Her response to this experience was, "When people have a problem with women in ministry, they need to take it up with Jesus. He is the One who put us there."[2]

These are just a few of the incidents that demonstrate the strong opinion in the Church on this critical subject. Opinions are diverse and strongly held, so I accept that there are those who will strongly disagree with what I am saying. I too have been in their position, but I feel like the man in the gospel of John who said, "Once I was blind but now I see."

Today's world

There is a vile evil in our world that seldom gets airtime on broadcast media, and for which, sadly, the Church must share some guilt.

A short while ago I was moved listening to Sheryl WuDunn speaking at the Leadership Summit at Willow Creek church in Chicago, USA. Together with Nicholas Kristoff she has written a book called *Half the Sky,* in which she states, "It appears that more girls have been killed in the last fifty years, precisely because they were girls, than men were killed in all the battles of the twentieth century. More girls are killed in this routine 'gendercide' in any one decade than people were slaughtered in all the genocides of the twentieth century." She also notes that women aged 15-45 are more likely to be maimed or die from male violence than from cancer, malaria, traffic accidents and war combined. Up to 70% of female murder victims are killed by their male partners.[3]

Women make up more than 50% of the world's population yet own less than 1% of its land, reveals Danielle Strickland in her book, *The Liberating Truth*. She also informs us that, "107 million females are effectively missing from the globe today, simply noted as 'missing.'"[4]

Both the Office for National Statistics and Rape Crisis report some sobering statistics which highlight the wicked evils perpetrated against women in our world today. In Britain,

- 45% of women have experienced some form of domestic violence, sexual assault or stalking
- Around 21% of girls experience some form of child sexual abuse
- At least 80,000 women suffer rape every year
- 1 in 5 women aged 16-59 has experienced some form of sexual violence since the age of 16

And around the world,

- One in three women is beaten, coerced into sex or abused in her lifetime
- Between 700,000 to 4 million women and children are trafficked for prostitution, labour and exploitation, with as many as 750,000 in the USA alone in the last ten years

- Female genital mutilation is practised in 29 countries with 135 million victims living with the consequences and 3 million at risk each year. It is estimated that 170,000 women and girls in the UK have undergone this barbaric ritual
- A UN Report claims that 90% of girls and women over the age of 3 were sexually abused in parts of Libya during the civil war
- We all know about the genocide in Rwanda. What is less spoken of is that in those 100 days, between a quarter and half a million women and girls were raped. In the Bosnian war it was up to 50,000; in Liberia about 49 per cent of the whole female population aged between 15-70. Rape has been used not just to satisfy desire, but as a tactic to destroy communities. Women are deliberately raped in front of their husbands, with terrible psychological and social consequences.[5]
- Loren Cunningham in his book, *Why Not Women?* states that, "No gender has been more aborted, abused, exploited, humiliated, persecuted, murdered and enslaved. From this generation alone, between 60 and 100 million girls are missing – killed by their families because of their gender."[6]
- The United Nations Website reports that three quarters of all the people living in poverty are women
- Women are 50% of the population but only own 1% of the world's wealth

Still, today, many churches enforce old, unbiblical paradigms, often without recognising it. I refer to the Marriage Service in which the question is asked, "Who gives this woman to be married to this man?" The statement points back to the deep-seated tradition that a daughter was the property of her father until given to be the property of another man. Today, in many evangelical wedding services, the vow of submission is a female-to-male arrangement only, which as we shall see is not supported by Scripture. The woman even has to surrender her name for her husband's. Many will see this simply as a cultural issue, but it goes much deeper. Since culture is reflected in its practices, this is one area of church life that requires urgent action, which in turn demands great courage from church leaders!

As a culture, and in the Church generally, women have been given the stereotypical role of "homemaker" and viewed as belonging in the kitchen; seen as the man's subordinate, only capable of domestic tasks, or given lesser roles than men. An example of this stereotype is seen towards the end of the 19th century when Elizabeth Garrett Anderson became the first lady to qualify to be a doctor (GP). She faced huge obstacles to making progress in her profession. Men would not go to her simply because she was female. Other women conformed to the way things were done then and continued seeing male GPs. It took years for Anderson to succeed. Even words from British Royalty have held back the empowerment of women, as seen in this statement from Queen Victoria: "Let women be what God intended, a helpmate for man, but with totally different duties and vocations."[7]

If further proof were needed that a misogynistic attitude towards women is embedded in society, consider the following quotes:

Prominent author Kurt Vonnegut said, "Educating a woman is like pouring honey over a fine Swiss watch, it stops working." Former Vice President of the USA, Spiro Agnew said, "Three things have been difficult to tame, the oceans, fools and women. We may soon be able to tame the ocean – fools and women will take a little longer." Former President of Poland, Lech Walesa delivered this shocking statement: "Women are to have fun with, in politics I prefer not to see a woman. Instead of getting all worked up, they should stay as they are, like flowers."[8]

Many strongly Jewish Orthodox men grew up having been taught to pray this prayer first thing each morning: "Blessed be He who did not make me a Gentile. Blessed be He who did not make me a woman. Blessed be He who did not make me an uneducated man or a slave." Many a Jewish wife would hear her husband thank God for not being Gentile, a slave or female! The stark conclusion was: a Gentile could convert and a slave be released, but the woman could only ever be a woman.

Throughout this book I aim to expose such thinking as unbiblical. One thing I have discovered with the Bible: if you already have a particular mind set or starting premise, whatever it may be, you can usually build an argument for it, producing "proof" texts to support it. All your arguments can sound logical, but of course if your starting premise is wrong, then no matter how logical they sound, the conclusion will also be wrong.

In spite of the wonderful redeeming power of the cross, in our world and much of the Church, women are still getting a raw deal and are suffering in a way that God never intended. In confronting this issue, I appeal that we would do so with love, not contention, and ask the Holy Spirit to lead us into all truth. Humbly, we have to admit that we *"know in part"* (1 Corinthians 13:9). We are all still learners on our spiritual journey with more revelation to come. We also remember that the final authority is not cultural or societal trends, but a proper understanding and interpretation of the Word of God. I believe strongly that much of what the church believes about women has come from culture and not Scripture.

I echo the words of Kris Vallotton in his book, *Fashioned to*

Reign, when he says,

"The most oppressed people group in the history of the world remains reduced within the Church. The world that Jesus died for empowers women. They can be mothers, doctors, astronauts, scientists, neurosurgeons, astrophysicists, teachers, sports analysts, athletes, fire officers, police officers, sailors, generals, entrepreneurs, detectives, artists, dancers, missionaries and so much more. Women can defend countries, start businesses, fight crime, create technology, rescue lives, put out fires and raise children. The Bible acknowledges women as queens, prophets, judges, teachers, mothers, leaders, apostles, co-heirs, counsellors, warriors and sons of God and much more. It is therefore confusing to me that somehow, in the Church that Jesus is the Head of, women are not qualified to talk, teach, shepherd or even help lead a congregation of thirty people. Something is wrong with this picture, and it is time that we got it right!"[9]

The Abolitionists fought to bring about an end to slavery and the Suffragettes fought to get votes for women. It is high time that the Church took up the fight to ensure that women have full equality in the body of Christ and are as unrestricted as men. This is not a feminist agenda, but a Kingdom agenda. Until it is so, the Church will not be fully equipped to play its vital role in God's plan of world redemption.

Endnotes:

1. Javier Moscoso, *Pain, a Cultural History* (Palgrave Macmillan, 2012), p97.
2. David Van Biema, *The Preacher's Daughter* (Time Magazine, May 1st, 2000), pp56-57.
3. Nicholas D. Kristof and Sheryl WuDunn, *Half the Sky* (New York: Vintage, 2010), p83.
4. Strickland, Danielle, *The Liberating Truth: How Jesus Empowers Women* (Monarch Books, 2011).
5. Kristoff and WnDunn, *Half the Sky* (New York: Vintage, 2010), p84.

6. Quoted in Loren Cunningham & Joel David Hamilton, *Why Not Women?* (YWAM Publishing, Seattle, 2000), p20.
7. Bingham, Colin, *The Affairs of Women* (John Gunn, 2006), p134.
8. Quoted in Loren Cunningham & Joel David Hamilton, *Why Not Women?* (YWAM Publishing, Seattle, 2000), p21.
8. Ibid p21.
9. Vallotton, Kris, *Fashioned to Reign* (Baker Publishing Group, 2013), p129.

CHAPTER 3
BACK TO
THE GARDEN

Those who teach the subordination of women to men often refer to the "creation ordinance" and base their view on five arguments from Genesis chapter 2 which run something like this:

- The woman was created after the man and is therefore secondary to him
- The woman is taken "out of" the man and so is inferior to him
- The woman is named by the man and therefore is under his authority
- The woman is made as a "helper" for man, which reveals him to be the head
- The woman tempted the man and so was responsible for the fall

In this chapter I want to show that each of these arguments is invalid because they begin from the wrong premise – as does much teaching about women.

Genesis is the book of beginnings and the seedbed of biblical truth. In other words, every truth in the Bible can be found in seed form in Genesis. To properly understand the role of both men and women, we have to go back to the beginning, where it is mentioned for the first time, and see God's original design and intention. In the first 3 chapters of Genesis we see four things very clearly.

1. Both man and woman came from the same soil

Genesis 1:26 says, *"Then God said, 'Let us make man in our image, in our likeness, and let them rule over the fish of the sea and the birds of the air, over the livestock, over all the earth, and over all the creatures that move along the ground.'"*

Although woman was made after man, she was not an afterthought. She was included in the "them" God referred to. "Adam" means "humankind" and the Hebrew word can be used for a person's name, the male gender, or for humankind without being gender specific.

Derek Tidball, former principal of the London School of Theology, in his book *The Message of Women* says, "God created in His image a male 'adam' and a female 'adam.' The word "Adam" is not used as a personal name until Genesis 4:25 and here is used generically as humankind."[1]

Genesis chapter 2 explains and expands on the creation narrative in chapter 1 in more detail. Everything we see in Genesis is described as "good" or "very good", until we come to Genesis 2:18, where God says, *"It is not good for man to be alone, I will make a helper for him."* How we read this is very important. The Creator does not have second thoughts and feel He had better give man some company, creating the woman as an afterthought. Making woman was ALWAYS God's intention (Genesis 1:26). When God talked about making humankind, He talked about making it in His own image. The image of God could not be reflected in maleness alone; it required femininity, since God is neither male nor female. He is Spirit, but He invested His image into mankind – His character, His values and moral qualities; not just in maleness, not just in femaleness, but in BOTH.

Another important aspect of the image of God is that He dwells in community as the Trinity, which has implications for us. Grenz and Kjesbo in their book, Women in the Church, pick up on this point:

"This understanding of the divine image constitutes a strong foundation for affirming the participation of men and women in all areas of church life. Because we are the image of God only as we share together in community, we must welcome the participation and contribution of all individuals, both male and female. Because men and women have unique contributions to make, the church must value the contributions of both sexes to the fulfilment of its task. No congregation can genuinely expect to complete the mandate given by the Lord if its structures only allow the male voice to be heard in planning and decision making. The wisdom and insights of both male and female are equally important to the on going ministry of God's people, for each gender's perspectives and experiences reflect quite different approaches to life."[2]

The image of God in the creation of male and female is primarily a relational concept. Men and women are different, but neither gender has the ability to fully reveal God's image alone. Any sense of man bearing the image of God and woman being inferior to him is absent from the biblical text and undermines the community of the Godhead.

It is interesting that throughout the Old Testament the Hebrew word for the Holy Spirit is *Ruach*, which is feminine in gender, but we don't consider the Spirit of God to be inferior to Father. The Holy Spirit has such feminine qualities that the early Church fathers referred to Him as "She"!

As Christians we believe in the Trinity, Father, Son and Holy Spirit, three persons in one God, who live in total equality as the

Godhead. In the same way, humanity consists of both maleness and femaleness – neither greater than the other, but both together, reflecting the image of God in humanity. So, in creating woman, God was not saying here is someone subordinate to the man; He was saying that there is something missing. Maleness alone was not a complete reflection of His image – femaleness was needed for that. Man and woman are both 50% of God's image. Together they make up 100% of His image in creation.

Notice too man and woman's shared origin. Adam was made from the dirt, but when God came to make woman, He didn't use more dirt. If He had, the woman's origin would have been similar, but different to the man's. Instead God makes woman from man – out of the same stuff from which He'd made Adam. They had the same substance, but were separate expressions of the same creation. Genesis 2:21 describes God taking a "rib" from Adam. The Hebrew word used occurs 42 times in the Old Testament, but this is the only occasion where the translators render it "rib". The Hebrew word literally means "side". In other words, God took man's "side" and from it made another "side". From the side of the man, He then made woman. Mary Evans in, Woman and the Bible rightly says, "...derivation is not a strong argument for subordination. It is wrong to say that woman owes all her existence to the man, just as it would be wrong to say that man owes all his existence to dust and is therefore subordinate to it. Both man and woman are portrayed as created directly by an individual and purposeful act of the Creator."[3]

The Bible says that woman was made to be "helper" for the man. That little phrase has incorrectly turned into a doctrine in the minds of those who believe it implies women exist to serve and support men. Picture me needing some help with my car. One person is a skilled mechanic who is able to repair it and make it run perfectly. Another person is someone who washes it for a couple of pounds. In relation to me and my car, I could describe them both as a "helper", but clearly one is greater than the other. Many read the phrase "helper" in Scripture and assume it describes an inferior role, but that is not what the text says.

If we look closely at the Hebrew word translated "helper", a much different picture appears. *Ezer* is used 21 times in the Old Testament. 72% of the time it refers to a superior, and it NEVER refers to a subordinate. 16 times the "helper" in question is God, such as in Psalm 121:1:

"I lift up my eyes to the hills – where does my help come from? My help comes from the Lord, the maker of heaven and earth."

This is the same word used in Genesis to describe the woman. When we speak of God as our helper, we understand that He is not inferior, but much greater than us. "Helper" indicates strength, not weakness or inferiority. The noun used here carries the picture of help in the form of "rescue, saviour, rescuer, protector". I believe a wrong understanding of this word "helper" has caused great damage to a proper understanding of the role of women when, in fact, the Bible says nothing that points towards inferiority or subordination.

Commentating on this Hebrew phrase *ezer kenegdo*, biblical scholar and theologian Victor P. Hamilton writes,

"It suggests that what God creates for Adam will correspond to him. Thus the new creation will be neither a superior nor an inferior, but an equal. The creation of this helper will form a one-half polarity, and will be to man as the South Pole is to the North Pole. She will be his strongest ally in pursuing God's purposes and his first roadblock when he veers off course."[4]

New Testament scholar Daniel Kirk concurs: "Only this kind of shared participation in representing God's reign to the world is capable of doing justice to the God whose image we bear."[5]

When God brings the woman to the man, Adam says in Genesis 2: 22, *"This is now bone of my bones, flesh of my flesh, she shall be called woman for she was taken out of the man."* Adam declared her to be equal, but different.

Notice that the woman was not called "Eve" until after the fall. The Hebrew word here for "man" is *ish* and the word for woman, *isha*, because she was taken out of *ish* (out of him). The Hebrew "adam" is used as a generic term for the man until the woman is created, at which point Adam refers to himself (Genesis 2:23) as *ish* and the woman as *isha*. In grammatical terms, he simply feminises the word for man, because the woman is the female version of the male. There is no inequality implied, just the opposite.

Psalm 139 teaches that all of us are *"fearfully and wonderfully made"*, having a shared origin and being made of the same stuff. The argument that man was made before woman and is therefore superior to her is a poor one. Goats and pigs were made before man!

2. Both man and woman were given the same mandate

A careful look at the job description given to man and woman, ish and isha (because they only became Adam and Eve post-Fall) is very revealing. They were given the same role by God, jointly and equally, with no hierarchy. Genesis 1:28 says, *"God blessed them and said to them 'subdue it .... Rule.'"*

The rule, leadership, dominion and government of the world was given equally to both of them. There is no hint that God gave man more authority than the woman, or that the woman was subject to the man. There was no restriction placed on the woman's role or extension of the man's role. The five responsibilities God delegated were given in the plural "you". Together they were given leadership over every living thing, over the sea, over all creation. Man and woman were joined with God in ruling the world.

Dr Gilbert Bilezikian writes in his excellent book, *Beyond Sex Roles*, "They are both equally entitled by God to act as his vice regency for the rulership of the earth. The lack of any restriction or of any qualification in their participation in the task, implied roles of equality for man and woman."[6]

Nowhere do we read that Adam was delegated the rulership of his wife, or that she is told to submit to him. Before the Fall, both roles in marriage were equal, with both parties serving the purposes of God side by side with equal Kingdom authority.

Some make a case for man's superiority over woman by pointing to the fact that Adam named the animals prior to the creation of woman (Genesis 2:19-20), such as Mary Kassian in her book, Women, Creation and the Fall. Kassian states that there is implicit authority in the act of naming something and argues that because Adam named the animals, it proves that men were ordained by God to be the leaders of the animals and of women.[7]

It is difficult to see the logic of Kassian's claim considering that the woman did not even exist at this point in time. There is no logical correlation between Adam naming the animals and his supposed authority over Eve and biblical scholarship provides no evidence that naming something is an indication of authority. Moreover, Genesis 1:27-28 says that both man and woman were given authority over the animals, not just the man.

Kassian also states that Adam, "...recognized his God-given responsibility and authority by naming the woman."[8] Then, without apparent logic, Kassian adds, "If the woman and man were meant to have identical roles, God would have named the woman, just as He had named the man."[9]

In fact, God did name the woman, just as He named the man. God named all human beings "adam" – "human beings" – and the man and woman called themselves "ish" and "isha" – the equivalent of Mr and Mrs.

Other highly gifted Bible scholars have come to some equally strange conclusions. William Hendriksen is a favourite of mine, yet I stagger at his words in his commentary on the Pastoral Epistles: "In His Sovereign wisdom God made the human pair in such a manner that it is natural for him to lead, for her to follow; for him to be aggressive, for her to be receptive; for him to invent; for her to use the tools which he invents. The tendency to follow was embedded in Eve's very soul as she came forth from the hand of her Creator."[10]

I challenge anyone to find that in Genesis 1 and 2. Just recently, Dr John Andrews, the Principal of Mattersey Hall was preaching in our local church and said "If you had turned up in the Garden of Eden prior to the fall, you wouldn't have known who the leader was." How true!

3. Both man and woman participated in the fall

It is astonishing how many assumptions are made when it comes to the disastrous Fall of mankind documented in Genesis 3. It is so easy to paint a picture that fits our view, rather than seeing what Scripture actually states. The woman is often painted as the seducer and temptress, but Eve was not alone when the serpent came. Genesis 2:6 states that the man was at her side when the serpent arrived and throughout the temptation, during which time he never said a word. Neither does the Bible say that the woman tempted her husband. As Victor Hamilton points out, "Eve is not presented as a temptress; the snake alone tempts. Hers is a sin of initiative. His is a sin of acquiescence. Adam and Eve are both caught up in the same moment, equally responsible and equally guilty."[11]

In Genesis 3:1 we read, *"The serpent said to the woman, 'Did God really say you must not eat from any tree in the garden?'"* In English, the word "you" can be single or plural depending on the context. In Hebrew, however, there are two different words, one singular and one plural. The "you" in Genesis 3:1 is plural. First of all the serpent acknowledges that God was speaking to both the man and the woman when He gave His command. Then the serpent uses the plural "you" when he replies. He was definitely speaking to both of them. The descriptive phrase, "She also gave some to her husband who was with her, and he ate it" confirms that he was there.

What is interesting is that the serpent recognised that the greatest resistance would come from the woman, not the man, so he spoke directly to her. In the end, both participated in the eating and both were guilty of the transgression.

Many of the distorted views of women that have crept in the Church originate from Babylonian Talmudic writings or Pagan Greek Philosophers, and these views have coloured our thinking when it comes to interpreting the Bible. So often the woman is cast as the villain of this piece, whereas read correctly the opposite is true. At least the woman put up a bit of a fight. At least she said a few things to the serpent about what God had said. The man never said a word!

Notice too that the man received God's command regarding what not to eat in the garden first hand, since the woman had yet to be created. The woman received the command "second hand" from the man. Yet, with only second-hand knowledge, she still put up some resistance.

After they had both sinned, God turns up and asks them,

"What have you done?" We see that the woman comes out best, admitting, *"The serpent deceived me"*, while the man shifts the blame: *"The woman YOU put here with me..."*. The man not only blamed the woman, he blamed God too!

Disobedience is worse than deception. While the woman was deceived, the man disobeyed. The New Testament puts the responsibility for what happened on Adam. Paul underlines his culpability in Romans 5:12-19 and 1 Corinthians 15:21-22. Any idea that sin entered the world because Eve usurped Adam's headship is absent from the Genesis narrative.

When God speaks following the Fall, notice that the man and woman are not cursed. Rather it is the serpent and the ground that are cursed (Genesis 3:14, 17), signifying the spiritual world and the natural world. What was spoken to man and woman were the consequences of their sin. God uses the word "shall" a number of times. This is not imperative, but future tense. In other words, God is not commanding something He wills, He is predicting the consequences that will occur as a result of their big error.

When God says, *"Your husband shall rule over you"* (or "will" rule over you in some translations), many take this to mean that it is God's will for women to be under the authority of men. Not so. God is saying that this will be one result of the Fall, stating the consequence of male/female inequality, not expressing His will. This "rule" was something new – it did not exist before the Fall. Genesis 3:16 does not describe the way God intended things to be.

Part of the consequences was a change in the man and woman's relationship. Verse 16 is difficult to translate: *"Your desire will be for your husband and he shall rule over you."* This is unlikely to mean sexual desire. Many commentators believe it to mean, "You shall desire the intimacy and unity you once enjoyed with your husband, but he will rule over you." God was not laying a foundation for inequality, but rather describing the consequence of sin.

In the 16th century John Calvin made an outrageous statement which many have been influenced by: "God commanded men to rule women and assigned women the role of obedience to men."[12]

This is completely unbiblical. Man's dominance of woman is a result of sin, not the will of God. The result of the Fall was the collapse of man and woman's equal relationship, after which would come a power struggle in which men and women would pay a huge price.

Gilbert Bilezikian sums it up by saying, "Adam became subject to the soil from which he was taken. Eve became subject to Adam, from whom she was taken. Adam's toil would make him slave to the ground that would eventually engulf his life. And Eve's life would now be ruled by the slave."[13]

It didn't take long for the consequences of the Fall to work their way through society. Within six generations we read about polygamy in Genesis 4:19, where Lamech married two women. God's original idea of equality had vanished and women were taking a lesser, inferior role. Women have been grossly exploited ever since. The only thing that has ever brought release to women subject to male exploitation is the Gospel of Jesus Christ.

4. Both man and woman received the promise of salvation

In Genesis 3:15: God said, *"I will put enmity between you and the woman, and between your offspring and hers, he will crush your head and you will strike his heel."*

The word translated "offspring" is actually "seed". The conflict would be between the serpent and the woman, because it would be the seed that came from her who would one day strike the serpent. It was a foretelling of the coming of Christ (see also Galatians 3:16,19). As Loren Cunningham put it in his book Why No Women?, "When we look at the issue of women and their role, we are entering humankind's most ancient battlefield, the war of the serpent against women."[14]

It is tragic that so many seem to want to restrict the redemption that flows from Calvary and somehow give women a lesser salvation than men. Both were given the same hope and we see in this verse that when it came to the deliverance of mankind, the woman would play the major role. The seed of the woman, not the man, would bruise the serpent's head.

Karl Ernst von Baer discovered the mammalian ovum in 1827, and Edgar Allen discovered the human ovum in 1928. So it wasn't until very recently that we understood what the woman contributed to the birth of a baby. Prior to that, people believed in preformationism (the theory that organisms developed from miniature versions of themselves). In other words, that male sperm contained miniature people and the woman was just the soil into which the seed was planted. We now know that the male and the female contribute 23 chromosomes each to make up a foetus. The Bible, however, teaches that all the human DNA of Jesus Christ came from the woman alone.

The issue of the subordination of women is as significant as the issue of slavery. For years Christians supported the idea based on a single phrase, occurring twice in Scripture, but taken out of context: *"Slaves obey your masters"*. It justified not only slavery, but racism too, and people had to fight long and hard to break the back of slavery. Similarly, women have been minimised and dominated through a misunderstanding of the Bible's teaching. As a result, the Church has lacked something vital. Throughout history homosexuals, women and slaves have often been considered less than human. In 584AD, in France, 63 Bishops and representatives met and voted 32 to 31 in favour of the motion "Are Women Human?" Women, declared human by one vote![15] It is literally beyond belief.

Two thirds of all Bible believing Christians in our world are women, yet a large number of the body of Christ are still shackled by untruth. It's time we renewed our thinking and turned the tide.

Endnotes:

1. Tidball, Derek & Dianne, *The Message of Women*, (Inter-Varsity Press, 2012), p34.
2. Grenz & Kjesbo, *Women in the Church*, (Inter-Varsity Press, 1995), p172.
3. Evans, Mary, J. *Woman in the Bible* (Inter-Varsity Press, 1983), pp15-16.
4. Victor P. Hamilton, *The Book of Genesis Chapters 18-50* (Erdmans, 1995).
5. Quoted by www.rachelheldevans.com/blog/mutuality on 4th June 2012.
6. Bilezekian, Gilbert, *Beyond Sex Roles* (Baker, 1985), p25.
7. Kassian, Mary, *Women, Creation and the Fall* (Crossway Books, 1990), pp19-20.
8. Ibid pp16-17.
9. Ibid p19.
10. Hendriksen, William, *Timothy & Titus* (Banner of Truth, 1957), p109.
11. Hamilton, V. P. *The Book of Genesis* (Erdmans, 1990), p200.
12. Parales, Heidi, *Hidden Voices* (Smith & Helwys, 1998), p2.
13. Bilezelien, Glibert, *Beyond Sex Roles* (Baker, 1985), p58.
14. Cunningham & Hamilton, *Why Not Women?* (YWAM Publishing, 2000), p15.
15. Walker, Grace, *Women are Defective Males* (Aardvark Global Publishing, 2010), p121.

CHAPTER 4
RESTORING EVE
AS WELL AS ADAM

In our search to understand how women should be treated in the Church, the community of believers, we must look to our ultimate role model and observe the way in which the founder and builder of the Church treated women. But before we examine how Jesus treated women, it is vital to understand how women were perceived and treated in the world at the time that He entered it.

2,000 years ago the Romans ruled Palestine. Greek was the universal language and Greek thought had permeated the world. Then there were the Jews, to whom Christ came first. These three worlds overlapped – Roman, Greek and Jewish cultures co-existing, side by side. I will give an overview of each, so that we can understand how, when Jesus came, He confronted each of them with the life and love of God.

Roman Culture
It was said that the Romans took cities, while the Greeks took minds. The Romans dominated through their military power and their conquests spread far and wide. In Roman society, a husband had absolute power over his wife. Girls were considered ready for

marriage aged 12-14, whilst it was 17-18 for boys. When a girl married, she was expected to give up her religion and worship the ancestors of the family she married into.

In Roman culture women did not have their own full name, but rather were identified by the feminine version of her father's family name (hence Julius Caesar's daughter was known as "Julia" because the family name was Julius). When a boy was born into a family, he was given an individual name, but girls were given the family name. To avoid confusion, if there was more than one girl they would be named "Julia 1", "Julia 2" and so on!

The lives of women were so devalued that it was common for them to be killed by family members as a punishment. The father of a household was allowed by law to kill his married daughter if she was caught in adultery, for instance.

Greek Culture

In Greek culture, girls married at 14-18, whilst men married in their twenties or thirties, which meant that the husband was often twice the age of his wife. Athenian law viewed women as inferior and subordinate to men, so they had no more legal rights than a slave. All women were under the guardianship of a man (referred to as their *kyrios* or "master"). Women had no significant participation in society, unable to own property or to control finances. Education was limited to the strictly practical – they were taught only what they were deemed to need to know, nothing more. Many Greek wives hardly left the home during their lives. Women were not allowed to eat in the same room as a man.

Though the Romans treated women as second class citizens, it was nothing compared to the Greeks. What many Christians fail to grasp is the extent to which this Greek mind set has influenced the Western world for nearly 2,000 years. Statements made by many Greek philosophers leave us in no doubt as to their opinions about women.

Aristotle (384-322BC) was the teacher of Alexander the Great who conquered the world. Through his conquests Alexander was able to spread Greek philosophy. In Why Not Women? Loren Cunningham quotes Aristotle:

"...female is a monstrosity – a deformed male, a deformity. The female sex has a more evil disposition than the male, is more cowardly and less honest, the male is by nature more superior, and the female inferior, the male is ruler and the female is subject."[1]

According to Aristotle the birth of a female was a necessary perversion of the "norm", which happened only to ensure the continuance of the species. Aristotle also studied bees and came to the conclusion that because a swarm of bees followed one bee, that bee must be male. Centuries later, of course, it was discovered to be a queen bee!

In his comedy Lysistrata, the playwright Aristophanes had a group of men chanting, "Women are a shameless set, the vilest creatures going."[2]

Similarly, Menander (341-291BC) said, "Women are an abominable cast, hated of all the gods." And "where woman is, there is all evil."[3]

The famous Greek statesman and lawyer Demosthenes said in a famous defence speech, "Mistresses we keep for the sake of pleasure, concubines for the daily care of our person, but wives to bear us legitimate children."[4]

Pythagoras taught that Adam would have remained happy and immortal if Eve had never come along.

Socrates said, "The male sex is far better than the female, being born a woman is divine punishment, since women are half-way between a man and an animal."[5]

Hippocrates, the father of medicine, also taught the inferiority of women: "...the nature of women is less courageous and weaker."[6]

Jewish Culture

Jesus was born of a Jewish woman, so what view was held of women in the Jewish culture of His day? Jews considered women to be so prone to sin that they needed male leadership/headship. They were marginalised in worship, being segregated from the men. In terms of education, rabbinic schools were solely for boys. In order to establish a Jewish synagogue, a quorum of 10 men was needed; women didn't count.

The Jewish historian Josephus, who wrote around the time of Jesus, said, "Women are inferior to men in every way."[7]

In the differing Talmuds (the oral law of the rabbis), we can see a clear prejudice against women, as the following selected quotes illustrate:

"When a boy comes into the world, peace comes, when a girl comes into the world nothing comes."[8]

"Rather should the words of the Torah be burned than be entrusted to a woman. Whoever teaches his daughter the Torah is like one who teaches her obscenity."[9]

One Rabbi said, "All women are nymphomaniacs" and another, "A woman is like a pitcher full of filth, with its mouth full of blood, yet all run after her." Yet another, "He who talks much with women brings evil upon himself"[10] and "All we can expect of them is that they bring up our children and keep us from sin."[11]

I remind you of the prayer that many Jewish men would pray each morning: "Thank you God that I am not a gentile; thank you I am not a slave; thank you I am not a woman."[12]

Into this world where men dominated, full of sinful proud

arrogance, where women were downtrodden and maligned came Jesus, the Saviour. At the beginning of His ministry Jesus, having been baptised and received the fullness of the Holy Spirit, went into the synagogue (Luke 4) and declared His mission mandate, quoting a prophecy about Himself from the book of Isaiah:

"The Spirit of the Lord is upon Me, He has anointed Me to proclaim freedom for the prisoners, to release the oppressed."

None were more oppressed than women in Jesus' day.

I am so thankful that this man, Jesus, was a different kind of man. In Luke's Gospel alone a third of the interactions we read of Jesus having were with women. Overall in the gospels 40 different women are mentioned – either in His teaching, or those with whom He had personal contact.

Gilbert Bilezikian writes, "The Gospels are unique in presenting a great variety of situations that involve women. Remarkably, not in a single case is a woman denigrated, reproached, humiliated or cast into one of the lewd stereo-types of the day. Males, especially establishment types, power-wielding men, are often the object of severe castigations, but not women. Jesus' treatment of women is always solicitous and supportive, as if He were assuming responsibility towards them for a long history of derogation and compensating for it with an outpouring of divine love."[13]

I will summarise in four way how Jesus related to women in His ministry, and came to restore Eve as well as Adam.

1. Christ Lifted Their Position

One of the most amazing incidents is found in Luke 13:10-17:

"On a Sabbath Jesus was teaching in one of the synagogues, and a woman was there who had been crippled by a spirit for 18 years. She was bent over and could not straighten up at all. When Jesus saw her, He called her forward and said to her, 'Woman, you are

set free from your infirmity.' Then He put His hands on her and immediately she straightened up and praised God. Indignant that Jesus had healed on the Sabbath, the Synagogue ruler said to the people, 'There are six days for work, so come and be healed on those days and not on the Sabbath.' The Lord answered him, 'You hypocrites, doesn't each of you on the Sabbath untie his ox or donkey from the stall and lead it out to give it water? Then should not this woman, a daughter of Abraham, whom Satan has kept bound for eighteen long years be set free on the Sabbath day from what bound her? When He said this, all his opponents were humiliated but the people were delighted with all the wonderful things He was doing."

This is perhaps the most powerful evidence that reveals how Jesus "lifted" the position of women to that of equality with men. Several things Jesus did in this account were extremely radical. Jesus was teaching in the synagogue when He saw the woman and *"called her forward"* (v12). Women were kept at the back of such meetings, behind screens. To call a woman forward in public was unthinkable. Religious gatherings were the domain of men. Then Jesus spoke to her as He publicly healed her. It was taboo for men to speak to women in public. But worse than this, in the act of healing Jesus put His hands on her. This was outrageous and would have brought gasps of shock and horror from the assembled men. Men did not touch women in public, let along in the synagogue. A woman could be divorced if she was touched by another man.

No doubt the place was in uproar and the synagogue leader protests to Jesus. But Jesus speaks perhaps the most radical words a Jewish man could ever utter about a woman. He calls her a "daughter of Abraham" (v16). Prior to Jesus, there is no record of this phrase ever having been used before. It was unheard of in Judaism. Men referred to themselves as sons of Abraham, but no one taught that women were daughters of Abraham.

So we see that not only did Christ bring healing to the bent over woman, causing her to stand up straight, He also restored her dignity and elevated her position to that of an equal standing with men. In this one simple statement Jesus affirmed that Jewish women were equal heirs of the promises of Abraham, along with Jewish men. The stigma and inferiority of womanhood was smashed and Jesus had scolding words for the male religious rulers: "hypocrities!"

I believe the same Jesus wants to do the same thing in His Church today. Even 2000 years later, there are numerous churches in many parts of the world where religion is still a man's world, where somehow women are not entitled to the same privileges, opportunities or blessings. It is time for the Church to broadcast the teaching of the New Testament in Galatians 3 which declares that all believers, both men and women, have equal status as "the children of Abraham". We are joint heirs with Christ – heirs of every Kingdom promise and every Kingdom blessing.

2. Christ Levelled Their Playing Field

In the Old Testament we don't read find a verb that means "to marry". Rather men "took" wives. The consequences of the Fall that God predicted were happening – women were suffering under the rule of men and they sought to impose their dominance in the marital relationship.

In the gospels there are five instances where Jesus deals with the subject of marriage. We notice that each time, the language He uses is one of mutuality and equality, never subordination or subjugation. In Mark 10:2-12 Jesus levels the playing field for the first time and teaches equality. The Pharisees came to Jesus in order to test Him, asking, *"Is it lawful for a man to divorce his wife?"* (posed entirely from the male perspective). Jesus answered their question with a question: *"What did Moses command you?"* They answered, *"Moses permitted a **man**..."* Jesus pointed out, *"It was because your hearts were hard that Moses wrote you this law."*

Now Jesus takes them back to God's original intention. *"But at the beginning* [Creation] *God made them male and female ... for this reason a man will leave his father and mother and be united to his wife, and they will become one flesh."* First, Jesus highlights that the man and woman are no longer two, but one, then adds: *"Therefore what God has joined together let **man** not separate."* Then in verse 10, Jesus the revolutionary says, *"Anyone who divorces his wife commits adultery against her, and if **she** divorces her husband and marries another man **she** commits adultery."*

Christians often use this passage to argue about marriage and divorce, but what we need to see here is that Jesus gives women the same rights as men – He does not differentiate between the two. Up until this point, the rights of betrothal and divorce were male dominated – that's how Jewish culture operated. But Jesus cuts across centuries of rabbinical teaching and puts man and woman on level ground. The Rabbis taught that a man could divorce his wife for almost anything. If she spoilt the dinner; if she talked too much; if she had bad breath; if he didn't like the size of her bosom. All these things are found in rabbinical writings. Suddenly, with a single stroke Jesus gets rid of all that nonsense and clarifies God's perspective: in divorce, as in marriage, it is the same for women as it is for men, because they are equals. Incredible! It is hard to understate what a revolutionary idea this was to His hearers – the same rules apply to BOTH.

John chapter 8 records the story of the woman caught in the act of adultery. The very statement of this fact is revealing. That she was caught "in the act" means there must have been a man with her at the time, yet "she" is caught, not "he" and not "them", even though they were both guilty. The law actually prescribed death for both parties by stoning, but the religious authorities were not applying the law fairly, favouring the male, so it was the woman alone who was dragged to the feet of Jesus.

Jesus challenges the men by once again levelling the field: only the person without sin may cast the first stone. In other words, the law applied to both men and women. The religious rulers were trying to make adultery a female-only sin. Not so, says Jesus.

In Matthew 5 we find another example of Jesus bringing balance and equality in the sermon on the Mount. In Palestinian Judaism it was taught that if a woman showed her face in public, she would cause a man to lust after her. In order to avoid causing a man to sin, she must keep herself covered up. One rabbi said, "If a man gazes at the little finger of a woman, it is as if he gazed at her secret place."[14] One class of Pharisee, known as the "Bleeding Pharisees" would walk around with their heads down, so as not to look at a woman. As a result they would often bump into things, hence their name! They believed that women were so seductive and prone to sin that you couldn't even look one in the eye without being entrapped. The prevailing view then, was that women were not only responsible for their own sins, but also for awakening lust in men! Jesus, however, would have none of this and placed the blame solely on the man. *"If **you** lust in **your** heart, **you** have committed adultery in **your** heart."*

Jesus challenged the culture of His day with grace, truth and divine authority.

3. Christ Loved Them Publicly

No one loved like Jesus. The society into which He was born looked down on women. They were downtrodden, seen as inferior, considered inadequate and the cause of much sin. But when Jesus came, women of all ranks, all classes, and from all walks of life received His attention. He interacted with married women, Gentile women, women considered unclean, demon possessed women and prostitutes. It didn't matter who they were, because Jesus conferred value and dignity on them all. In doing so He broke every taboo in society – He touched them; He gave them a voice in public. His actions were revolutionary and astounding. He ignored the cultural barriers and publicly expressed love for all these women in a way no one had ever seen before.

In John chapter 4 we read the account of the Samaritan woman at the well. Jesus ignored and cut across a 500 year old hostility between Jews and Samaritans. Jesus spoke to this woman (which was culturally unacceptable) who was from a despised racial minority (which was bad) and belonged to a fringe religious sect (which made it worse). On top of all this, the woman lived an immoral life and had had five husbands. No respectable Jew would have been caught talking to her in public, but Jesus asks her for a drink. In fact, this account is the longest recorded conversation Jesus had with anyone in the gospels. Even more amazing is the fact that He engaged her in a theological discussion. This might not seem remarkable, but remember that in Jesus' day doctrine was not taught to women because they were deemed to be incapable. It was considered an obscene waste of time. Jesus spent more time teaching doctrinal truth to this woman than He did the religious ruler Nicodemus in the previous chapter. He also imparted wonderful revelation to her:

"God is a Spirit, and they that worship Him, must worship Him in Spirit and in Truth."

How amazing that He chooses to share such wonders with

a woman others considered a "low life". The Samaritan woman received, even before Peter, the revelation that Jesus was the Messiah. Jesus didn't treat women as second class citizens. He came to seek the lost – men and women alike. In verse 27 we read that the disciples arrived and *"...were surprised to find Him talking with a woman..."*. It was a history changing moment. It was also a life changing moment for the woman. Overwhelmed with the revelation she had received she rushed back into her village to spread the news and became the first evangelist in the New Testament. Yes, a woman! Scripture records that, *"Many of the Samaritans of that town believed on Him because of the woman's testimony."*

Luke 7:36 is perhaps the most extraordinary scene of interaction between Jesus and a woman – and the most flagrant to those persecuting Him. At Simon's house He allows a prostitute to unbind her hair (forbidden in Jewish culture as it was seen to be provocative and sexually enticing, and also grounds for divorce if a man's wife uncovered her hair in public). Jesus allowed the woman to speak to Him publicly, and then touch Him publicly, anointing Him – both of which, but especially the latter, were unthinkable. The reaction of Simon and the others was typical of their culture and they would have expected Jesus to rebuke her for her outrageous behaviour. Instead He honoured her sacrificial expression of love for Him, dignifying and blessing her. In fact, instead of rebuking the woman, he rebuked Simon in his own house, using her as an example!

"You see this woman ... I came into your house, you did not give me any water for my feet, but she washed my feet with her tears and wiped them with her hair. You did not give me a kiss, but this woman from the time I entered has not stopped kissing my feet. You did not put oil on my head, but she has poured perfume on my feet.

Therefore I tell you her many sins have been forgiven, for she loved much, but he who has been forgiven little, loves little."

4. Christ Loosed Them Powerfully

Those who argue against female Christian leaders often refer to the fact that Jesus had 12 disciples, all of whom were men. But there were female disciples, even though they were not amongst the twelve. Luke 8 tells us that, *"The twelve were with Him, and also some **women** who had been cured of evil spirits and diseases."* It was unprecedented for a teacher to have women travelling with him as disciples. There is no record anywhere of a rabbi having female disciples, apart from the gospels!

In Luke 11 we are introduced to Mary and Martha. Several things that we may overlook in this scene would have surprised first century onlookers. First, Mary was sitting in the male occupied part of the house, rather than in the back room with any other women. This was part of Martha's big problem – the fact that Mary had cut across one of the basic social conventions. Second, Mary sat at Jesus' feet. This phrase in Greek is the same one used to describe Paul sitting at the feet of Gamaliel, his teacher. The person doing the sitting was training to become a rabbi themselves.

So Mary took the posture of a disciple, the place of a learner. Notice that whilst others wouldn't dream of teaching a woman, Jesus was different. He was adamant that, *"It will not be taken from her."* It may have been the first time ever that a woman was allowed to be taught in this way. Through this Jesus set a precedent. As Tom Wright comments, "Examples like Mary's, no doubt, are at least part of the reason why we find so many women in positions of leadership, responsibility and initiative in the early Church".[15]

Luke chapter 8 reveals another interesting fact, referring to several of Jesus' female disciples by name:

"...*Mary from whom seven demons had come out. Joanna, a wife [married woman] whose husband was the manager of Herod's household, Suzanna and many others. These women were helping to support them out of their own means.*"

What is really interesting here is that women were financing the ministry of Jesus. Joachim Jeremias comments that women leaving their homes to follow Jesus was "an unprecedented happening in the history of that time, so Jesus overthrew custom when He allowed them to leave home and follow Him."[16]

Again in Luke 24:22, the disciples on the Emmaus road make reference to *"certain women of **our** company...".* It was given that women formed part of Jesus' group of disciples. Jesus released women to serve Him just as He did men. To Martha, He gave the revelation that He is the "resurrection and the life" and her response was to confess, in the Greek, exactly the same words as Peter, *"You are the Christ, the Son of the living God"* (John 11:27). When it came to women Jesus had no double standards. There were no exclusions and no limits on their destiny. At a time when, legally speaking, a woman could not be trusted as a reliable witness to a crime, God chose a woman to be the first witness of Christ's resurrection. A woman was the first to testify to the resurrection whilst the male disciples were still trying to comprehend it.

Tom Wright says, "Mary Magdalene and the others are the apostles to the apostles. If an apostle is a witness to the resurrection, there were women who deserved that title before any of the men!"[17] All Christian ministry begins with the announcement that Jesus has been raised from the dead – and God first entrusted that task not to Peter, James or John, but to Mary Magdalene.

John Stott writes, "Without fuss or publicity Jesus terminated the curse of the Fall, reinvested woman with her partially lost nobility and reclaimed for His new Kingdom community, the original creation blessing of sexual equality."[18]

Dorothy Sayers puts it well when she writes,

"Perhaps it is no wonder that the women were first at the cradle and last at the cross. They had never known a man like this man – there never has been such another. A prophet and teacher who never nagged at them, never flattered or coaxed or patronised; who never made arch jokes about them, never treated them as 'the women, God help us' or 'the ladies, God bless them!'; who rebuked without querulousness and praised without condescension; who took their questions seriously; who never mapped out their sphere for them, never urged them to be feminine or jeered at them for being female; who had no axe to grind and no uneasy male dignity to defend; who took them as He found them and was completely unselfconscious. There is no act, no sermon, no parable in the whole Gospel that borrows its pungency from female perversity; nobody could possibly guess from the words and deeds of Jesus that there was anything 'funny' about women's nature."[19]

When the men had forsaken Him and fled, the women were still there at the cross. No wonder, because this man Jesus had treated them like no other man. It is hardly surprising that there is not one record of a woman ever speaking against Jesus in the gospels. Jesus treated them with love, teaching, healing, and without contempt. For this He had no parallel in the two centuries prior to His birth or in the century in which He lived.

Endnotes:

1 Cunningham & Hamilton, *Why Not Women?* (YWAM, 2000), p77.

2. Ibid. p79.

3. Ibid. p79.

4. Doriani, Dan., *Woman and Eloquence* (Crossway Books, 2003), p72.

5. Bristow, John T., *What Paul Really Said About Women* (Harper Collins,1991), p4.

6. Cunningham & Hamilton, *Why Not Women?* (YWAM, 2000), p80.

7. Hurley, James B., *Man & Woman in Biblical Perspective* (Wipf & Stock, 2002), p61.

8. Swidler, Leonard, *Biblical Affirmations of Women* (Westminster John Knox Press, 1979), p157.

9. Trombley, C., *Who Said Women Can't Teach?* (Bridge–Logos, 2003), p40.

10. Swidler, Leonard, *Biblical Affirmations of Women* (Westminster John Knox Press, 1979), p156-157.

11. Meeks, Wayne A., *In Search of the Early Christians* (Yale University Press, 2008), p34.

12. Barrs, Jeram, *Learning Evangelism From Jesus* (Crossway Books, 2009), p39.

13 .Bilezikian, Gilbert, *Beyond Sex Roles* (Baker, 1985), p82.

14. Cunningham & Hamilton, *Why Not Women?* (YWAM, 2000), p103.

15. Wright, N.T., *Surprised by Scripture* (HarperOne, 2014), p70.

16. Jeremias, Joachim, *Jerusalem In The Time Of Jesus* (SCM, 1969), p376.

17. Wright, N. T, *Surprised by Scripture* (HarperOne, 2014), p69.

18. Stott, John, *Our Social and Sexual Revolution* (Baker, 1999), p110.

19. Cunningham & Hamilton, *Why Not Women?* (YWAM, 2000), p112.

CHAPTER 5
PUTTING WOMEN
IN THEIR PLACE

I heard of an incident some time ago which illustrates how we tend to think of certain roles as gender specific. A plane was sat on the runway awaiting permission to take off when a voice came over the sound system saying, "Good morning ladies and gentlemen, my name is Susie and I'm your captain on this flight." An audible gasp and nervous laughter rippled through the aircraft. This story carries a profound lesson. Wouldn't most of us prefer a competent female pilot than an incompetent male? Of course we would! Why then, in church life, is gender so often put before gift?

In many churches that have the position of senior minister, it is usually assumed this role must be filled by a man. As a result of this policy, sometimes the role is filled by someone simply because they are a man, even if their gifting is not sufficient for the role. A woman might be better equipped and more suited to the role, but is overlooked because of her gender. There are other churches that will only ever appoint male deacons and elders. (Ironically, men will often go home and pour out to their wives what has been discussed in oversight meetings, to gain their wisdom!)

Cultural stereotypes like this exert a powerful influence on us that are hard to resist, especially in the Church. Anyone who has ever assumed responsibility for leading a church will know how hard it is to change things that are a long-established part of the fabric, and yet every renewal demands change and cannot occur without it. Scripture is unchanging, but our understanding and interpretation of it will often be challenged as we receive new light. Once I was blind regarding the topic of this book; I passionately preached the Bible, but certain views I held were skewed by prejudice and personal bias. I look back now with shame that I didn't encourage my wife or daughters to live beyond the stereotypical female roles that were thrust upon them.

Jesus didn't expect anyone to conform to the stereotypes imposed by society, and He didn't conform Himself. In His time women were the carers of children, but Jesus picked children up and put them on His knees. Women performed domestic duties, especially the preparation of meals, but Jesus cooked a meal for His disciples. Only women or servants washed people's feet, but Jesus did this too. When we are freed of the gender issue, men as well as women are released.

As we consider in this chapter the place of women in the Bible we must bear in mind what John Ortberg refers to as the "preponderance" of Scripture. In other words, its "surpassing influence". It means that when we find a passage of Scripture that appears not to agree with other parts of Scripture, we can't make a doctrine from it, taken out of context. We must seek to understand it within the entire framework of the scriptural truth. When people build a doctrine on one isolated truth, this is how we fall into error, and where the roots of cults are found. For example, it could be said, based on Ephesians 6:5 – *"Slaves, obey your earthly masters with respect and fear"* – that the Bible supports the concept of slavery. Indeed, many Christians justified slavery based on this verse for generations until others saw the light and fought to see it abolished.

Those who fought to see slavery ended did so on the *preponderance* of Scripture, seeing the bigger picture of the sanctity and freedom of every human being.

In a similar way, those who fail to recognise gender equality do so whilst glibly quoting isolated pieces of Scripture, seeking to build an entire doctrine when they only have a few pieces of a much larger jigsaw. They ignore the preponderance of Scripture.

Putting Women in Their Place in The Old Testament

Contrary to what is often thought, the Old Testament honours women. Nowhere do we find the teaching that women possess inferior status. Neither does the Old Testament teach the culpability of women, particularly with regard to the Fall. Even in the Ten Commandments God says we should, *"Honour your father **and mother"***. Parents were to be equally obeyed – there was no sense that one party was superior to the other. Let's look at several other Old Testament examples.

Abraham is known as the father of our faith, the patriarch from whom all believers come. The Bible tells us how God chose Abraham and changed his name from Abram to Abraham to better reflect his destiny. But it's easy to miss the fact that God did exactly the same for Sarah. He chose her and changed her name from Sarai to Sarah to reflect her destiny. *"No longer call her Sarai, her name will be Sarah, I will bless her"* (Genesis 17:15). Just as Abraham became the patriarch, Sarah was the "mother of nations" and kings would come from her.

God used women to fulfil positions of leadership in the Old Testament, who had His authority to bring the word of the Lord into situations. Who can miss the powerful influence of Miriam? If I asked you to recall who led the Children of Israel out of slavery, you would probably refer to Moses and Aaron. You would only be two-thirds correct! Israel, consisting of some 2-3 million people, were led by a leadership team of three: Moses, Aaron and Miriam. Micah 6:4 says, *"I sent Moses to lead you, also Aaron and Miriam."*

God appointed Miriam to lead because she had the right combination of character and gifting. Elsewhere she is identified as a prophetess who speaks the word of the Lord. Exodus 15:20 also shows that she was the first worship leader in the nation's history and the "song of Moses" in this chapter may well have been composed under her inspiration. In Numbers 12:15, when Miriam had leprosy because of a judgement by God upon her, the entire nation could not even move until she had been restored. Some might discredit Miriam's leadership for doing something wrong, but remember that Aaron made a serious error too, leading the people into idolatry with the golden calf. Miriam's sin was envy – and her slip up had nothing to do with her being a woman. Moses too made an error and failed to enter the Promised Land as a result. The fact is, Miriam was a great spiritual leader; she was not a raving feminist, she was a woman chosen and raised by God to do a specific job according to His will. Each of the three person leadership team had a clear, complementary role: Moses was lawgiver, Aaron was priest, Miriam was prophetess.

Then there was Deborah. She is referred to as a prophetess, a judge and a military leader. It is impossible to read about Deborah without feeling great admiration. Judges 4:4 records the fact that she was leading Israel at that time. She was to her generation what Moses was to his. Deborah was an incredible leader who joined with a general called Barak in defeating the Canaanite army. Israel's victory came because God used Deborah to deliver His word and to instruct thousands of soldiers to go to battle. Her courage and submission to the Lord were critical factors in bringing peace to the nation for 40 years. If you read

Judges chapters 4 and 5, you'll notice that when Deborah delivers the battle strategy to Barak, he will not go unless she comes with him. In the words of Scot McKnight, "Deborah led the nation spiritually, musically, legally, politically and militarily."[1]

Deborah's courage was remarkable and her zeal and passion continue to inspire many today. The old argument that, "God used her because there were no men available at the time" is an insult to the Lord! In Proverbs 8 God says of Himself, *"By me kings reign and rulers make laws that are just. By me Princes govern and all nobles who rule on earth."* In other words, *all* leaders/rulers are positioned by Him. To say that God somehow had to break His own will in order to use a woman makes no sense. God raises up whom He desires because He has called and equipped them for His purposes. If He chooses to use a woman, then He is free to do that. His ways are not our ways. Those who argue that Deborah was used because Barak was weak need to look at Hebrews 11:32 where Barak is praised for his faith.

Rather than commanding women to remain silent in religious gatherings, the Old Testament calls forth their voices. In Psalm 68:11 we read, *"The Lord gives the word and a host of women bring the good news."* Just as Deborah was identified as a prophetess, so Huldah was recognised as possessing this gift. Though Jeremiah, Nahum, Habakkuk and Zephaniah were all prophesying around the same time, Huldah is consulted regarding the word of the Lord to Israel (2 Kings 22:12-20). Huldah stood out as a prophetess who was unafraid to speak God's words and, as a result, there was a great revival under King Josiah. Huldah did not defer to any male leadership, but took responsibility for hearing and bringing the word of God herself. Isaiah also described his wife as a prophetess.

Esther was an outstanding woman whose courage saved a

nation. She risked her own life to see God's purposes prevail. God could easily have positioned a male deliverer if He had chosen to do so, but He did not.

There are many more names that could be mentioned. I have focused on just a few. However, it is clear that God has always used women to lead with authority and to bring the word of the Lord. There is no mention that women in leadership is an aberration of God's will or any sense that it is wrong.

Proverbs 31, one of the most cherished passages of teachings in the Bible, was given to King Lemuel by his mother. More than a thousand verses of Scripture have come from the lips of women. God inspires women to speak His word, just as He inspires men. Paul taught Timothy that, *"All scripture was given by God for … teaching"* (2 Timothy 3:16). It follows that if God can inspire women to speak the word of the Lord, He can certainly use them to teach it.

Finally, there is a lovely verse in Nehemiah 3:12 that says, *"Shallum, son of Hallohesh, ruler of a half-district of Jerusalem, repaired the next section **with the help of his daughters**."* Women were engaged in executing God's purposes alongside the men. They certainly did not fit into the complementarian stereotype as they helped to rebuild the walls of Jerusalem! In summary, there is no notion in the Old Testament that there is anything wrong with female leadership.

Putting Women In Their Place In The First Century

One of the opening scenes of the New Testament leaves us in no doubt as to God's pleasure in positioning women for His purpose. The first statement of faith in the New Testament comes from the lips of a woman, Mary. *"Be it unto me, according to your word"* (Luke 1:38). Mary, the mother of Christ, played a huge role in

God's redemptive plan. Tasked with giving birth to and raising the Saviour, Mary would have been His educator as well as His nurse. Her wonderful "magnificat" in Luke1:46-55 reveals something of the Spirit's revelation to her. What is also often missed is that the events of the first two chapters of Luke could only have been relayed to Luke by Mary herself. It is also worth noting that the angel didn't ask Joseph or her father for permission to speak with Mary, he just went directly to her.

Mary immediately responds with faith. This is how Smith Wigglesworth puts it,

"As we receive the Word of Life, it quickens, it opens, it fills us, it moves us, it changes us, and it brings us into a place where we dare to say 'amen' to all that God has said. There is a lot in an 'amen.' You never get any place until you have the 'amen' inside of you. That was the difference between Zacharias and Mary. When the Word came to Zacharias, he was filled with unbelief until the angel said *'You will be mute … because you did not believe my words'* (Luke1:20). Mary said, *'Let it be to me according to your word'* (v38). The Lord was pleased that she believed and there would be a performance of what He had spoken. When we believe what God has said, there will be a performance."[2]

When the baby Jesus was taken into the temple, it was a prophetess, Anna, at this defining moment in human history, who was given the task of announcing to the world the arrival of the Messiah. Anna is the only prophet mentioned in the inter-testament period – a woman!

Women in the Early Church

The role of women in the early Church gives us further evidence regarding their equal status with men. Let's look at the day of Pentecost.

Jesus' disciples were gathered together, men and women, in the upper room. That day they *all* received the same baptism of power. They *all* received the same soaking, the same burning; they *all* spoke in tongues and *all* declared the wonders of God. Some might protest that Acts 2:7 only speaks of this happening to men, but this is only because some translations have added in the word "men". In the Greek text the word is absent. God did not keep women silent on the day of Pentecost; they received the full flame of the Holy Spirit!

I love how Scot McKnight describes the Day of Pentecost: "Pentecost was the day the music of the Fall died and the day new creation music began to be sung."[3] Hallelujah!

Note that when Peter got up to preach he quoted from Joel: *"I will pour out my Spirit on all people, your sons and daughters will prophesy..."* (Acts 2:17). If God has declared that both men and women will speak by divine inspiration, then it cannot be right that women should remain silent.

Events surrounding the persecution of the early Church by Saul give a glimpse into how strategic women were at that time. Ken Bailey, who spent his life working in the Middle East, comments on how women were free to come and go during the crucifixion episode – just as happens today in troubled regions such as Lebanon; whilst men are fighting, woman carry on doing the shopping, taking children to school etc. After the death of Stephen in the book of Acts, however, we see women being targeted just as the men are. Bailey notes that this only makes sense if women were also seen as leaders and influential figures within the community.

In Acts 21, Phillip's four daughters prophesied. There were also women teachers in the early Church who were accepted, endorsed and affirmed.

Priscilla and Aquilla were a husband and wife team; leather workers and itinerant church planters who partnered with Paul in Ephesus and Corinth. Both in Rome and Corinth they are seen hosting a church in their house. They are mentioned seven times in the New Testament. On five of those occasions Priscilla's name comes first, contrary to the common practice of the day (see Acts 18:2-3, 18, 19, 26; Romans 16:3; 1 Corinthians 16:19; 2 Timothy 4:19). The King James Bible erroneously reverses the order of the original Greek in order to correct this "scandal", but Priscilla's name appears first and most Bible commentators agree that it was she who had the prime role in their ministry. Just as in English the accepted way to refer to a couple is Mr and Mrs, it would be uncommon to render "Mrs and Mr" unless a particular point was being made.

Some may argue that Priscilla taught in the home, but not in the church. But we must bear in mind there were no church buildings at the time, so this is a flimsy argument. As Linda Belleville is quoted as saying in *Two Views on Women in Ministry*, "Such distinctions are decidedly modern ones."[4]

For the record, the fact that Priscilla had the lead role in their ministry, does not make her husband Aquilla any less of a man. They just had different roles. In stark contrast, in this twenty-first century, Karen Lowe, the senior leader of a church in Wales, makes comment in her book on the Welsh revival how her husband has been criticised over the years for standing back and encouraging her to take the main leadership role in their church. She writes that some even questioned his manhood, simply through him supporting his wife in reaching her full destiny, according to the gifts God has given her.

Yet God has no problem at all with such an arrangement. It was accepted by the early Church that Priscilla was the more gifted teacher, though both her and her husband taught. Priscilla taught Apollos, who was a Bible teacher himself (Acts 18:26), but needed some help in his teaching and doctrine.

The Apostle Paul acknowledges the fact that Priscilla helped establish churches in Corinth, Ephesus and Rome. Priscilla and Aquila led churches in their own home, but Priscilla was the main spiritual leader. John Chrysostom, a fourth century Church Father credits Priscilla for being both the teacher of Apollos and the pastor of the church in Corinth after Paul moves on.

The Issue of the Female Apostle

In Romans 16:7 Paul makes mention of another couple who have been key figures in the establishment and strengthening of the early Church. The text says, *"Greet Andronicus and Junia."* The 1946 Revised Standard Version of the Bible (as well as many other modern texts) changed the name to "Junias", making it male, and unfortunately added *"**men** of note among the apostles."* This made it seem that Paul was talking about two men, but in fact the original Greek text identifies the second person as Junia, a woman. The 1984 edition of the NIV also incorrectly rendered Junia as Junias, but later editions have corrected this.

The core reason for the uncertainty is simply that scholars and translators battled with the fact that Junia – identified by Paul as an apostle – was a woman. Complementarians such as John Piper and Wayne Grudem state that we cannot know whether this person was in fact a man or a woman, claiming that "the evidence is inconclusive."[5] But the opposite is true and I believe Piper is utterly wrong on this. Junia is undeniably a woman's name. If we dig deeper, there is no historical evidence of a "Junias" having existed. As Pierce and Groothius write, "The masculine name Junias does not occur in any inscription, letterhead, piece of writing, epitaph or literary work of the New Testament period. The feminine Junia, however, appears widely and frequently. Perhaps the best-known example is the half-sister of the famed Roman general Brutus."[6]

Why is "Junia" such a hot issue? Because if it's true that she was indeed a female apostle, then she must have taught in the church and also appointed men as leaders, having authority over them. As David Williams says in his excellent self-published book, *Junia: a Woman, an Apostle*, "I wonder if it would be possible to find an example of a person in the Bible who is only mentioned once, who has been argued about more than, or even as much, as Junia."[7]

Those who hold to the views of complementarianism or patriarchy somehow have to bury Junia to make their case watertight. The easiest way is simply to make her a man!

In his book on Romans Simon Ponsonby writes, "Twentieth-century evangelical translations, with all the weight of tradition to influence interpretation, struggle to conceive of a woman as an apostle. However, we must heed the witness of a natural Greek speaker who would better grasp the meaning of Paul's text, writing in the fourth century, Bishop Chrysostom. He was quite clear that Junia referred to a woman and an apostle: 'And indeed to be apostles at all is a great thing. But to be even amongst these of note, just consider what a great eulogy this is! But they were of note owing to their works of achievement. Oh! How great the devotion of this woman that she should be even counted worthy of the appellation of apostle.'"[8]

In all probability, Andronicus and Junia were another husband and wife team, like Priscilla and Aquila, but Junia was also held to be an apostle – the highest office in the New Testament Church – and an "*outstanding*" one at that. As Andronicus and Junia are the only apostles mentioned in this chapter, some have suggested that they could even have been the founders of the church in Rome, such as Professor Francis Watson in *Did a Woman Found Roman Christianity?*[9]

Eldon Jay Epp has produced an outstanding study called, *Junia: The First Woman Apostle.* In it he argues that the unanimous, credible testimony of the Church's first millennium identifies Junia as a woman. The case for Junia being a woman is clear to those who are unbiased with no agenda.

Epp shows that Aegidius of Rome (AD 1243-1316) is the first reliably documented instance where Junia's name is converted to a man's name. Aegidius was among the first to record that both Andronicus and Junia were men. The change took place in approximately 1298, during the reign of Pope Boniface VIII (Benedict Gaetani, who reigned from 1294-1303). The Catholic Encyclopaedia goes on to tell us that this pope was accused of infidelity, heresy, simony, gross and unnatural immorality, adultery, magic, loss of the Holy Land, the death of Celestine V, and more. When King Philip IV of France brought these charges against him, five archbishops, twenty-one bishops and some abbots sided with the king! This evil man had persuaded the pope before him, Celestine V, to resign, and then following his own election as pope, imprisoned the elderly man until his death.

Until this evil man tampered with Holy Scripture the identity of Junia as a female apostle had been unquestioned for 1200 years, but from then on the masculine form "Junias" was introduced into the Bible, based on historic prejudice and the assumption that a woman could not be *"outstanding amongst the apostles"*.

Complementarians such as Piper and Grudem have a real problem here, as their argument for restricting women in ministry falls apart if Junia really was an apostle in the early Church.

Some have argued that Junia could not have been an apostle because Jesus didn't appoint any women to be part of the twelve, but this is a short-sighted argument. By that reasoning, no Gentiles could ever be apostles either.

For any reader wanting to study Junia in more depth, David Williams book *Junia: a Woman, an Apostle* is a good place to start. In it he expertly exposes the weaknesses in the views of Wayne Grudem and John Piper in their work, *Recovering Biblical Manhood and Womanhood*, which in my view has only served to reinforce the restriction placed on many gifted women in the body of Christ.

The Issue of the Female Deacon

In Romans 16 Paul also makes mention of Phoebe. In the English texts translators have rendered her role as that of a "servant", but the Greek word used is actually *diakonos*, commonly translated "deacon". Paul actually applies this title to himself, Apollos and Timothy; all three are *diakonoi* as well as apostles. Simon Ponsonby writes,

"The term 'deacon' is a masculine noun, though it was a description of a role that could be held by a woman – in this case, Phoebe. It just won't do, as some have tried, to suggest that when we read '*diakonos*' applied to men we are to think in terms of an official church leader, teacher and minister, but when we read it ascribed here of Phoebe, we are to think of someone like a "table-waiter". It would be more scripturally consistent that we think of Phoebe as a minister of the church in Cenchreae."[10] In those days women directed their own households, so when churches began to form in houses, many women became the leaders of these local "house churches".

The word "deacon" is mentioned twenty-two times in the

New Testament and is always masculine, even though here it is applied to a woman. This fact should also be borne in mind when we consider the word "elder". The term "deaconess" did not get invented for several hundred years after Paul wrote his letter, so we see Phoebe identified as a *diakonos* (deacon) using the male version of the noun. Paul describes Phoebe as an impressive leader whom he trusts to take his letter to the Romans. In those days, anyone who delivered a letter also had the job of explaining its contents to those who received it. This was Phoebe's task – the first commentator on the book of Romans!

When Paul writes that he "commends" Phoebe, the meaning of the Greek is "I stand with". In other words, Paul had great confidence in her. He calls upon the Romans to receive her and treat her as a leader. The English translations have traditionally downplayed her role saying, "she has been a great help to many...". Help is a weak word in English. The original Greek word translated "help" is *prostatis* – a very strong word. Josephus used this word in his writing when he referred to Caesar as the "*prostatis* of the universe", and it means "governor" or "ruler". The word is always used to describe one who has authority. It occurs only once in the New Testament, here in Romans 16:1. Liddle and Scott's Greek Lexicon defines *prostatis* as "a front-rank man, a leader, chief or administrator, or a president or presiding officer; or one who protects – a guardian, champion or patron."

There is no question then that women had authority in the Church. Paul underscores it by including himself as one who has been under her leadership, since the term is only used of someone acting with authority, such as kings, rulers, governments and so on.

Other New Testament Women of Influence

Paul mentions other women in Romans 16 who, he says, "work

hard for the Lord". Verse 6 mentioned Mary and verse 12 refers to several others. The church at Philippi had two key women in major leadership positions, Euodias and Syntyche, and Paul refers to them as *"fellow labourers"* (Philippians 4:2). The fact that they are named shows their seniority in the church in Philippi.

Paul commends Timothy's mother and grandmother for having taught him the Scriptures. Timothy's father was Greek and would not have known the biblical texts, hence his mother and grandmother were responsible for teaching him. Note: how could Paul commend women for teaching here, but state elsewhere that women should not teach? The preponderance of Scripture must be taken into account.

Chloe was a leader in one of the house churches in Corinth (1 Corinthians 1:11). It was from this house group that news came to Paul of quarrels. Hence Paul writes a response to Chloe's house, which brings that first epistle to the Corinthians.

F.F. Bruce says that Paul named a total of 39 people as colleagues in the ministry. 29 were men and 10 were women. Paul makes no distinction between the men and women who made up his fellow workers. Men and women alike received his praise for their collaboration in the gospel ministry, with not even the hint of a suggestion that there was any distinction between one or the other in respect of their status or function.

The authors of *Discovering Biblical Equality*, co-edited by Pentecostal theologian Gordon Fee, confirm that studies into Paul's use of language when referring to male and female colleagues is exactly the same, regardless of gender – a point that is endorsed by Catherine C. Kroeger, who says that, "…one of the best kept secrets in Christianity is the enormous role that women played in the early Church."[11]

Putting Women In Their Place In Church History

A study of Church history and the role of women over the last 2000 years reveals that women have played significant roles, but also that this has not been reported as well as men's contribution. Where women have fulfilled a significant, God-appointed role, they have often done so in the face of male prejudice. Women have been a constant target of the enemy, who has sought to hold them back from being fully released into the work of God. Since two thirds of believers in the worldwide Church are women, this should come as no surprise. If the devil can persuade us to side line and marginalise women, then he has neutralised two thirds of the Church.

That is why this is a very crucial topic indeed. If you look at early Church writings, material written between the first and third century after Christ contains nothing that restricts or demeans women in any way. After the first three centuries, however, demeaning references about women begin to appear and suddenly women in the Church becomes a controversial topic. After that, attitudes towards women quickly deteriorate.

Historical evidence verifies that the ministry of women was prevalent during the first centuries and it wasn't until the council of Laodicea in 363AD that women were prevented from being elders. The same council banned the Eucharist or breaking of bread from taking place in people's homes. The decline continued into the middle ages, marking the "Dark Ages", until the bright dawn of the Reformation. It was in those first few centuries, three or four hundred years after Christ, that the "wheels came off" the Church. Clergy became professional, the laity were side lined and, most crucially, women were marginalised and ultimately barred from leadership.

These are some of the disturbing thoughts of the Church

fathers, whose influence contributed to the marginalisation of women in the Church:

Origen: "It is not proper for a woman to speak in church; however admirable or holy what she says may be, merely because it comes from female lips."[12]

Tertullian, writing that every woman carries the curse of Eve, said, "You are the devil's gateway, you are the unsealer of that (forbidden) tree; you are the first deserter of the divine law; you are she who persuaded him (Adam) whom the devil was not valiant enough to attack. You destroyed so easily God's image, man."[13]

He also said that, "Woman is a temple built over a sewer."[14]

And, "In pain shall you bring forth children, woman, and you shall turn to your husband and he shall rule over you. And do you not know that you are Eve? God's sentence hangs still over all your sex and His punishment weighs down upon you. You are the devil's gateway; you are she who first violated the forbidden tree and broke the law of God. It was you who coaxed your way around him whom the devil had not the force to attack. With what ease you shattered that image of God: Man! Because of the death you merited, even the Son of God had to die … Woman, you are the gate to hell."[15]

Chrysostom: "For those things which I have already mentioned might easily be performed by many even of those who are under authority, women as well as men; but when one is required to preside over the Church, and to be entrusted with the care of so many souls, the whole female sex must retire before the magnitude of the task."[16]

And again, "The whole of her bodily beauty is nothing less than phlegm, blood, bile, rheum, and the fluid of digested food … If you consider what is stored up behind those lovely eyes, the angle of the nose, the mouth and cheeks you will agree that the well-proportioned body is merely a whitened sepulchre."

This bile is breath taking! As Marina Warner has written, "Godly women throughout the last two thousand years have had to endure such vile and aggressive opposition, yet even so, many have made their mark on the building of Christ's Church."[17] But there is more to come…

The Christian theologian, Saint Clement of Alexandria, wrote, "[For women] the very consciousness of their own nature must evoke feelings of shame."[18]

Saint Augustine, Bishop of Hippo Regius (354-430): "Woman does not possess the image of God in herself but only when taken together with the male who is her head, so that the whole substance is one image. But when she is assigned the role as helpmate, a function that pertains to her alone, then she is not the image of God. But as far as the man is concerned, he is by himself alone the image of God just as fully and completely as when he and the woman are joined together into one."[19]

Saint Albertus Magnus, a Dominican theologian of the 13th century: "Woman is a misbegotten man and has a faulty and defective nature in comparison to his. Therefore she is unsure in herself. What she cannot get, she seeks to obtain through lying and diabolical deceptions. And so, to put it briefly, one must be on one's guard with every woman, as if she were a poisonous snake and the horned devil … Thus in evil and perverse doings woman is cleverer, that is, slyer, than man. Her feelings drive woman toward every evil, just as reason impels man toward all good."[20]

Thomas Aquinas, Doctor of the Church, 13th century: "As regards the individual nature, woman is defective and misbegotten, for the active force in the male seed tends to the production of a perfect likeness in the masculine sex; while the production of woman comes from a defect in the active force or from some material indisposition, or even from some external influence."[21]

Protestant Reformers who particularly have shaped the last five hundred years of Protestant history have been no less condemning of the female gender:

Martin Luther, Reformer (1483-1546): "The word and works of God is quite clear, that women were made either to be wives or prostitutes."[22]

He also said, "No gown worse becomes a woman than the desire to be wise."[23]

And again, "Men have broad and large chests, and small narrow hips, and more understanding than women, who have but small and narrow breasts, and broad hips, to the end they should remain at home, sit still, keep house, and bear and bring up children."[24]

John Calvin, Reformer (1509-1564): "Thus the woman, who had perversely exceeded her proper bounds, is forced back to her own position. She had, indeed, previously been subject to her husband, but that was a liberal and gentle subjection; now, however, she is cast into servitude."[25]

* * *

Even after the Reformation, the Church struggled to release women to fulfil their destiny. In Celtic Christianity in the early centuries in Britain, there were a number of key women leaders, but when the King of Northumbria decided to place the Church under the Catholic Church, women were once again side lined. The Catholic Church, which doesn't allow women priests, admits that over half their missionaries are women, which adds to the ecclesiastical contradiction.

When the Reformation came, non-conformist denominations

were birthed in England in the early 17th century and the English Baptist Church began to use women to preach the word of God. The Quakers, through founder George Fox, strongly defended women in ministry. Surprisingly, for the times, Fox had strong egalitarian views and, based on the practice of the early Church, held that all God's people were called to ministry. During the 1640s-50s women were teaching, preaching, leading worship and evangelising on a large scale, with Margaret Fell a key leader of that movement. Whilst Margaret was in prison in Lancaster Castle in 1666 for holding religious meetings, she wrote a book – the first by a woman since the Reformation pleading for the recognition of the spiritual equality of men and women. She held that the opposition to women speaking came from a spirit of darkness that had been on the Church for 1200 years. She wrote, "So let this serve to stop that opposing spirit that would limit the Power and Spirit of the Lord Jesus, whose Spirit is poured upon all flesh, both sons and daughters, now in His Resurrection."[26]

Another well known Baptist preacher was Mrs Attaway, who in 1645 preached to over a thousand people in London each afternoon. Sadly, the all too common pattern of opposition followed and a century later the role of women in the Baptist Church was limited. It wasn't until 1925 that the Baptist Union Council officially accepted the call of women to lead churches.

Methodism also released women in ministry. John Wesley initially struggled with the issue, even though he allowed women to participate fully in his class meetings. He gave women leaders permission to "exhort", but instructed that they call their classes "prayer meetings" so as to avoid their short exhortations being misconstrued as sermons. However, these gifted women had great success, which caused Wesley to conclude that a woman's call was the key factor in determining her ministry. Even though it caused some hostile public opinion, Wesley publicly affirmed and encouraged women to preach. Probably the biggest impact on Wesley's attitude to women's ministry was his mother, who preached to 200 women every week in prayer meetings she led. Her influence was greater than that of Wesley's father who was a vicar. Unable to deny the fruit of his mother's ministry, Wesley said, "Since God uses women in the conversion of sinners, who am I that I should withstand God."[27]

The Methodist movement witnessed the ministry of women like Sarah Crosby who, in 1777, rode 960 miles, held 220 public meetings, 600 private meetings and wrote 116 letters. It was very apparent that she was one of the leaders of the revival. Another was Grace Murray, who Wesley referred to as "a servant and friend, and fellow-labourer in the gospel." Elizabeth Tonkin too was one of 27 noted women preachers in that exciting time in British history. However, as with the Baptists, within a short time and especially after the death of Wesley, women preachers were repressed with the Methodist Conference of 1803 referring to the preaching of women as "unnecessary" and "generally undesirable."

Anyone who reads Church history with an open mind cannot fail to see that whenever God moves, women are released in fruitful ministry. But then it seems that the male institution kicks in and launches a process that puts women back on the periphery of church life.

In the 19th century Charles Finney invited women to preach, pray and speak in public. He founded Oberlin College, the first college in America to allow women to study alongside men (and also the first to be racially integrated). Finney was the first Protestant leader to train women in theology and in 1853 one of his students, Antoinette Brown, became the first ordained woman in America.

The late nineteenth century evangelist Phoebe Palmer won over 25,000 people to Christ. She came to Britain from the USA in 1859 and, during a four year period, toured the country with her husband preaching powerfully in revival meetings. Because of the opposition to women preachers, she called her messages "talks", and even defended her position by writing a book called, *The Promise of the Father*, in which she stated that women were present on the day of Pentecost and, along with the men, their utterances were anointed by the Holy Spirit.

Palmer also stressed the idea that God could and would give the blessing of holiness in an instant to a believer, and taught that holiness could be gained by faith. This teaching gave rise to the Holiness Movement, which by 1900 had changed the beliefs and practices of almost every evangelical church in America and Britain. Her ideas shaped the early Pentecostal movement and the modern Charismatic movement of which I am glad to belong. The impact of her ministry cannot be over-stated.

Palmer had a great influence on Catherine Booth and the Salvation Army. Catherine, raised in a Methodist home, had read the Bible through ten times by the age of twelve and would not have seen anything like the ministry of Phoebe Palmer. She admired her greatly and when Palmer was being attacked, Catherine wrote a pamphlet in 1860 called, "Female Ministry; or Women's Right to Preach the Gospel". Her views were even stronger than Palmer's as Rosie Ward points out:

"In contrast with Phoebe Palmer, Booth did not argue that women should be associated with the domestic sphere, and wrote that if men had been freed from the curse of working in the field, then women should be freed from being confined exclusively to the kitchen. She then turned to the Bible passages often used in connection with women's preaching. Her arguments drew on her conviction that the first coming of Christ had made gender irrelevant in the Church."[28]

Catherine stated that the wrong interpretation of the passage *"let the women keep silent in the churches"* had "...resulted in more loss to the Church, evil to the world and dishonour to God than any other errors we have referred to."[29]

William Booth vowed never to oppose women preaching again after hearing a Mrs Buck preach in London. He fully supported his wife in her ministry, whilst also raising eight children. He encouraged his wife to preach, which is how the Salvation Army came to release women into ministry. One of his well known phrases was, "Some of my best men are women."[30]

The founder of the China Inland Mission, Hudson Taylor, employed effective women evangelists, noting that, "at Pentecost, God did not arrange a special women's meeting."[31] How true that is!

C. T. Studd said of his Africa Mission (now WEC) that two of his most effective churches were, "manned by women". He also wrote that a cannibal, who was reputed to have eaten over 100 men, was converted to Christ by a woman.

There are many, many other outstanding women throughout history who have been greatly used by God: Joan of Arc, Kathryn the Great, Kathryn Kulman, Mother Theresa, Amy Carmichael, and countless unnamed others.

Women also played a key part in the Welsh Revival. Young teenage women travelled with Evan Roberts as part of his mission band. Roberts also encouraged women to preach. Women were anointed by the Holy Spirit and free to minister until the ubiquitous pattern occurred and they were side lined in favour of male clergy. A similarly sad thing occurred following the Azusa Street Revival of 1906. Lucy Farrow, who had introduced William

Seymour to the baptism in the Holy Spirit, became a respected female leader in the revival. Within ten years, however, the role of women was restricted and limited by the male leaders.

Another outstanding example is Aimee Semple McPherson, the first woman ever to preach on the radio, who pioneered her own Christian Radio Station in 1924 with millions hearing and reading her printed sermons. From the age of 4 she stood on street corners and attracted crowds by reciting Bible stories. In an age when women were not even allowed to vote, she built a 5,000 seat facility, debt free, in Los Angeles during The Great Depression. Aimee founded the Foursquare denomination which began in 1923 and wrote 175 songs and hymns. Her preaching drew great crowds and the signs and wonders that came from her ministry caused the American Medical Association to investigate the claims, with the result that they found the claims "genuine, beneficial and wonderful." *Time* magazine named her as one of the most influential people of the 20th century. She ran great social welfare and feeding programmes for the poor and gained great favour in her city. All this at a time when her own life was filled with personal pain and tragedy.

Her first husband died soon after they moved to China to be missionaries, leaving her eight months pregnant. Her second and third marriages ended in divorce. She received many death threats and was kidnapped for a ransom three times. Aimee suffered from sickness most of her life and eventually died at the age of 54 from an accidental overdose of pain killers. However, she left an incredible legacy. In a lecture to one of her Bible School classes, she stated: "This is the only church, I am told, that is ordaining women preachers. Even the Pentecostal churches, in some cases, have said, 'No women preachers'. But I am opening the door, and as long as Sister McPherson is alive, she is going to hold the door open and say, 'Ladies, come!'" She was evidently true to her word, for by 1944, the year of her death, women accounted for 67% of the ordained clergy in the denomination which she founded.

By the beginning of the 20th Century there were 40 Evangelical Missionary Societies all led by women. Women missionaries were the first to translate the Bible into hundreds of language groups, mainly in the most difficult areas of the world. One writer stated, "The more difficult and dangerous the work, the higher the ratio of women to men." Astonishing! Twice as many women as men went as missionaries into China. Today in China, 80% of all the house churches are led by women. The renowned missionary Gladys Aylward was turned down by every missionary society, so this little woman went to China on her own and powerfully wrote some history!

Edith Blumhofer asserts that, "In the early Pentecostal movement, having the 'anointing' was far more important than one's sex. As evangelistic bands carried the full gospel across the country, women who were recognised as having the anointing of the Holy Spirit shared with men in the preaching ministry ... A person's call, and how other believers viewed it, was far more important than ministerial credentials."[32]

Both the Assemblies of God and Elim movements in Great Britain were influenced and impacted by the ministry of Spirit-filled women, something that continues today. The Assemblies of God in the USA are leading the way, as their latest figures (2015) show that 23% of all of their ministers are female. If the current trend continues it will soon be 50%. For over 20 years the number of credentialed women has been growing incrementally and they are beginning to see women serve their districts as executive officers.

The largest church in our world today (three quarters of a

million people) is the Yoido Full Gospel Church in South Korea led, until recently, by Dr David Yonggi Cho. Loren Cunningham (founder of Youth with a Mission) relates a story of visiting Cho. Yonggi Cho's mother-in-law was a great Bible preacher, but he said he could not use her because women could not teach in South Korea. Cunningham told him, "Put her in your pulpit." Then Cunningham suggested that his own mother (who had been a great influence on Cho) should be invited to preach at Cho's church as a guest speaker. Cho agreed and she preached in his church. After that Cho was encouraged to release his own mother-in-law to preach. That saw the beginning of thousands of women being released into ministry at Yoido Full Gospel Church, which today has over 1,000 full time Senior Pastors, and tens of thousands of assistant pastors. Many of them are women. When people asked Cho what was the secret of his church he told them, "Release your women."[33]

Women in the Church should be in the same place as men – that is, free to serve in any area, according to their gifting. The body of Christ must come to a place where we recognise that it is not gender that determines destiny, but gifting. It is as simple as that. Once we come into alignment with the clear teaching of the Bible, we will unshackle two thirds of the body of Christ.

The question needs to be asked, "Where are the women evangelists today?" The answer is that many are sitting in churches carrying divine gifts which are unopened, unused and overlooked. If a sober reminder is needed, hear the words of Florence Nightingale who wanted to be a missionary:

"I would have given the Church my head, my hand, my heart. She would not have them."[34]

Endnotes:

1. McKnight, Scot, *The Blue Parakeet* (Zondervan, 2008), p169.

2. Wigglesworth, Smith, *Daily Devotional* (Whitaker House Publishing, 1999).

3. McKnight, Scot, *The Blue Parakeet* (Zondervan, 2008), p191.

4. Gundry & Beck, *Two Views on Women in Ministry* (Zondervan 2001/2005), p59.

5. Piper & Grudem, *Recovering Biblical Manhood and Womanhood* (Crossway Books, 1991), p79.

6. Pierce & Groothius, *Discovering Biblical Equality* (InterVarsity Press, 2004), p117.

7. Williams, David, *Junia: a Woman, an Apostle* (2014), p11.

8. Ponsonby, Simon, *God is For Us* (Monarch, 2013), quoted on p436.

9. Watson, Francis, *A Guide to the New Testament* (Barnes & Noble book imports, 1987), p6.

10. Ponsonby, Simon, *God is For Us* (Monarch, 2013), p432.

11. Kroeger, C., "The Neglected History of Women in the Early Church" (www.christianhistoryinstitutue.org, 1998).

12. Swidler, Leonard, *Jesus was a Feminist* (Sheed & Ward, 2007), p260.

13. Swidler, Leonard, *Biblical Affirmations of Women* (Westminster John Knox Press, 1979), p346.

14. Ibid. p346.

15. Ibid. p346.

16. Schaff, Phil, *World Religions Made Easy* (Hendrickson, 1995), p40.

17. Warner, Marina, *Alone of All Her Sex* (OUP Oxford, 2013), p59.

18. Saint Clement of Alexandria, Christian theologian (c150-215), *Pedagogues II*, 33, 2.

19. Miles, A. I., *Violence in Families* (Augsburg Books, 2002), p53.

20. Goff, Stan, *Borderline Reflections on War, Sex & Church* (Lutterworth Press, 2015), p67.

21. Bell, Lynda A., *Visions of Women* (Human Press Ltd, 1983), p103.

22. Scanlon, Bethany K, *Occupy* (Planet Teach Publications, 2011), p82.

23. Ibid. p82.

24. Ibid. p84.

25. Baker, Melanie, M., *Life Lessons from the Garden of Eden* (Virtualbookworm.com Publishing, 2004), p86.

26. Routledge, *Women Imagine Change* (Routledge, 1997), p465.

27. Jaynes, Sharon, *What God Really Thinks About Women* (Harvest House Publishers, 2010), p117.

28. Ward, Rosie, *Growing Women Leaders* (Bible Reading Fellowship, 2008), p 83.

29. Ibid. p84.

30. Gariepy, Henry, *Christianity in Action* (Eerdmans, 2009), p36.

31. Ponsonby, Simon, *God is For Us* (Monarch, 2013), p437.
32. Goll, Jim W., *Father Forgive Us* (Destiny Image Publishers, 2000), p106.
33. Cunningham, Loren & Hamilton, David J., *Why Not Women?* (YWAM, 2000), p67.
34. Ibid. p25.

CHAPTER 6
A "BLACK &
WHITE" ISSUE?

In later chapters we will look in detail at some of the "controversial" verses that form the heart of the debate regarding the role of women in ministry, leadership and church life. Before we do, I want to pause and remind us of the ground rules. It is vitally important we bear in mind the principles of interpreting Scripture – which will not only help us understand these passages, but all of the Bible.

Christians must learn how to interpret properly all passages of Scripture. Biblical "hermeneutics" simply provides the rules or guidelines for interpretation. I am going to begin by outlining those rules. If we jump straight into the text without considering other factors – which is what people often do – we will end up with a wrong understanding.

In his book *For Such a Time as This*[1], Martin Scott mentions six principles that we need to remember when seeking to understand Scripture:

1. Recognise the Inadequacy of the "Flat Book" Approach
The flat book approach is where people quote Bible verses without

any attempt to understand either their context or their wider use in Scripture. For example, someone will quote "...*an eye for an eye and a tooth for a tooth*...". The Bible does say that in Exodus 21:24, but using the flat book approach – taking it out of context – one might conclude that it's acceptable to take revenge on someone by beating them up. Though these words are in the Bible, its says much more than that. We can't just lift that verse off the page and speak it out foolishly – "God said it, so that's enough for me!" As Loren Cunningham states, "mindless repetition of Scripture is no sign of true knowledge."[2]

Although the Bible is the inspired word of God, if we wrongly interpret it then we end up with something that is not inspired at all. That's why the Bible itself speaks of *"rightly dividing the word of truth"* (2 Timothy 2:15). The flat book approach doesn't respect the whole of God's word. Cults quote from the word of God, but their interpretation of the truth is faulty, so the results are faulty too. It is possible to know the Bible from cover to cover and still be spiritually lost.

We cannot therefore approach verses like *"women, keep silent in the church"* with a flat book mentality, ignoring the context and the larger picture of Scripture. To do so is to lift that verse off the page and miss the other sacred truths that make that verse look very different. It is not enough to know what the Bible says; we must know what the Bible actually means.

2. We Must Recognise That the Historical and Cultural Setting is Important

This principle is hard for some people to grasp. The entire Bible is God's word, but not everything in the Bible is God's word *for all time*. Please read this carefully. If we don't apply this principle to our interpretation we can end up making doctrines out of Bible verses that were intended only for a specific place and time. Some commandments clearly are God's word for all time. Others are clearly not. Some biblical truths are trans-cultural, while others are merely cultural i.e. they were relevant to their time and context.

Take an example from Genesis 17:10: *"Every male among you shall be circumcised."* Yes, the Bible says that, although I cannot ever recall hearing a sermon on how to have a successful circumcision! It is not a message for today, even though it's in Scripture. We have to interpret it in the light of its historical and cultural setting. There is much more that the Bible has to say that explains why we don't need to observe this ritual today.

There are numerous other examples. Deuteronomy 22:9 says, *"Do not plant two kinds of seed in your vineyard."* Leviticus 19:19: *"Do not wear clothing woven of two kinds of material."* Most reading this will be contravening that particular biblical command. Leviticus 25:36 says, *"Do not take interest of any kind from your countrymen."* If you have an interest-earning bank account you are breaking that one. You get the picture. There were cultural reasons for these rules in their historical context.

The Bible then contains truths which are temporal as well as eternal. Our challenge is to identify which is which and to act accordingly. If we try to turn a temporal truth into a truth for all time, we end up with legalism. If we take an eternal truth and try to make it temporal we end up with liberalism. We have to be careful – the historical and cultural setting is important.

F.F. Bruce was asked, "How do you interpret 1 Timothy 2:9-15 which suggests that women are not to teach?" and reputedly, his entire reply was, "It is merely a statement of practice at a particular time." In other words, it was never intended to be applied to ALL women in ALL places at ALL times.

As N. T. Wright says, "We must think and pray carefully about where our own cultures, prejudices and angers are taking us, and make sure we conform, not to any of the stereotypes the world offers, but to the healing, liberating, humanizing message of the Gospel of Jesus."[3]

3. We Must Recognise That "Unclear" Text Should Be Interpreted in the Light of "Clear" Text

Everyone accepts that there are verses in the Bible that are clear and other verses that are not so clear. Certain verses in Daniel or Revelation may leave us wondering, but other verses are easily understood. Hence, our starting point is critical.

Behind every question of faith and practice is a pre-supposition or a premise. If we base our belief system on an incorrect premise or pre-supposition, we may well build a logical argument, but we will end up with an incorrect conclusion. In ancient times, for example, people believed that our world was flat. Based on this premise, people argued that if one sailed too far, you would fall over the edge. It was a logical argument, but the conclusion was wrong because the premise was flawed – as Christopher Columbus bravely discovered. Likewise in Scripture, if we start with the wrong premise, even though our arguments are logical, we end up with the wrong conclusion.

There are around a hundred passages in the Bible that are clear in affirming the role of women in leadership, but fewer than half a dozen that are less clear and appear to be in opposition. Those who want to build an argument against women in leadership focus on the few unclear verses and ignore the many clear ones which endorse women's roles in the Church and Kingdom. We must take note of the teaching of all Scripture; the Bible must be understood in its entirety, with Christ always at the centre.

4. We Must Recognise That We Must Not Make Scripture Say More Than it Does

There is always the temptation to use Scripture to support a particular view that we hold, but we mustn't try to make the Bible say what we want it to say. In a previous chapter we discussed the use of the word "helper" to describe woman in the creation narrative. Many people turn to this word helper to support the view that women are subordinate to men, yet a correct understanding of the Hebrew word forbids such a view. We have to be careful not to make the Bible say more than it actually does.

Others hold the view that Eve was the cause of sin in the world because she was deceived, but the Bible does not actually say that. In 1 Timothy 2:12-14 Paul does indeed say, *"I do not allow a woman to teach ... and it was not Adam who was deceived, but the woman was deceived..."* but we cannot view this statement in isolation, taken out of context, or use it to support a particular view we have – we have to examine the rest of Scripture. At the time Paul wrote those words, the Church was being plagued by a group of women who were spreading gnostic teaching and leading others astray. More on this later, but for now we cannot read Paul's words and deduce that there is a general weakness in women that makes them more susceptible to deception than men. There is plenty of anecdotal evidence that proves this is not the case. Most of the world's cults were started by men: the Jehovah's Witnesses – Charles T. Russell, Mormons – Joseph Smith, the Moonies – Jim Jones etc.

As well as avoiding reading into the Bible, there are times when we have to admit we just don't know what a verse really means. We may read lots of opinions about it, but receive little biblical insight. It is better to admit we don't know than to try to make the Bible fit our theories.

5. "Teaching" Text Must Take Precedence Over Both Descriptive and Corrective Text

For example, passages in Ephesians and Romans lay out for us verse after verse of doctrinal systematic theology, giving clear teaching on justification by faith, imputed righteousness, propitiation, the cross, the resurrection and similar truths. But in addition to this clear doctrinal teaching there will be descriptive text (which is outlining the practices of New Testament church life) and corrective text (where specific local difficulties are being addressed).

Paul wrote the first letter to the Corinthians mainly to address some specific problems. It is mostly corrective. When Paul wrote his letters, he didn't have in mind that he was creating a doctrinal treatise that would dictate how Christians should live in our day. Though his words were God-inspired, Paul was writing to specific individuals or churches about specific situations that had to do with the culture of their day. Moreover, Paul was responding to letters he had received. In other words he had first-hand information which is withheld from us. We are not privy to the letters sent to Paul from the church at Corinth, so we must study as much as we can about the local context so that we don't misinterpret Paul's teaching and end up imposing rules on ourselves that God never intended.

6. We Must Recognise That We Need to Use Scripture Consistently

It is important that we don't fall into the trap of using parts of the Bible to prove our case whilst ignoring other parts. If we apply it, we must apply it consistently. For example, it is inconsistent to prevent women from fulfilling certain roles in the church on the basis of one or two verses, whilst ignoring other verse relating to women. 1 Peter 3:3 discourages women from wearing nice clothes and jewellery, and having braided hair, for instance. There are many churches that do not allow women to teach, lead or have authority, but those same churches don't ban women from having nice clothes, jewellery and hair-dos. Surely that is hypocritical? We can't take the bits of the Bible that suit us and apply them, whilst ignoring the rest. This is totally inconsistent and brings God's work and His word into disrepute.

I hope you will apply these principles and bear them in mind as we examine what the Bible teaches about women in more detail.

Endnotes:

1. Scott, Martin, *For Such a Time as This* (P. S. Promotions, 2000), p89.
2. Cunningham and Hamilton, *Why Not Women?* (YWAM, 2000), p31.
3. *The Biblical Basis*, a conference paper for the Symposium, Men, Women and the Church, St John's College, Durham, September 4, 2004 by the Bishop of Durham, Dr N. T. Wright.

CHAPTER 7
A TALE OF TWO
CITIES: CORINTH

In the next two chapters we will look in detail at the main verses that have been employed to restrict women's involvement in the Church. Before getting into the text itself, just a little more background context is necessary. The church in Corinth was founded by Paul in around 50-51 AD. Corinth was the largest city in Greece, a cosmopolitan port at the intersection of trade routes between Asia to the east and Rome to the west. About 100,000 people lived there. It was a thriving sea port with two large harbours and was a strategic place for trade, including its infamous sex trade, which was particularly welcomed by sailors and travellers. Sex and drunken debauchery was an obvious and open part of its culture.

The city was dedicated to the goddess Aphrodite, who the Romans knew as Venus. The great temple located in Corinth was infamous throughout the world for its prostitution. There were around 1,000 prostitutes whose services were used in their "sacred" worship. Corinth was a hotbed of immorality, since so much of its economy was dependent upon prostitution. A modern word to describe Corinth would be hedonistic. It was steeped in fleshly indulgence, drunkenness and debauchery. The name Corinth became synonymous with immorality.

It took two years to establish the church in Corinth and Paul was helped by husband and wife team Priscilla and Aquilla, as well as Timothy and Silas. The congregation came from a variety of backgrounds – Roman, Greek, Jewish converts, slaves and free people – and included some who had come to faith from pagan, hedonistic backgrounds. In 1 Corinthians 6 Paul recites a list of sinful activities and says, *"and such were some of you."*

The combination of people from diverse backgrounds and the pervading influence of immoral Corinth, meant that, consequently, the church had a lot of things going on that Paul needed to deal with. There was incest, partisanship, questions about eating meat from the markets that had been previously offered to idols, and some believers still having sexual relations with prostitutes. All these things are covered in Paul's letter. Amidst all of this, Paul spends more time on the issue of gender than in any of his other letters.

As we read Paul's letter, it is helpful to remember how women were viewed in Jewish and Greek culture at that time. Women could not vote; they weren't allowed to speak in public; marriages were arranged; women were not considered credible witnesses and could not testify in a court of law. In addition, in Jewish culture women were expected to dress modestly in accordance with Talmudic teaching, and head coverings were compulsory. Raised a Pharisee, Paul would have been strongly influenced by these teachings, yet following his conversion it appears that he turned his back on such practices, following the radical pattern of Christ.

It should also be remembered when reading these difficult passages that Paul is referring to things which both he and his hearers understood, but which we do not have access to.

The Issue of Headship

The opening verses of 1 Corinthians 11 form a passage that has been the source of heated debate in the Church for a very long time. When reading them, we must realise that there were no chapter divisions in the original Greek text. Translators introduced them in order to make verses easier for us to locate. The words that end the previous chapter are therefore important. We read at the end of chapter 10, *"Whether you eat or drink or whatever you do,* ***do it all for the glory of God.*** *Do not cause anyone to stumble. I am not seeking my own good but the good of many so that they may be saved – follow my example."* Earlier Paul has said, *"everything is permissible, but not everything is beneficial"* (v23) and *"nobody should seek his own good, but the good of others"* (v24).

So when we come to the verses of chapter 11, and Paul's statement on headship, we understand that the thrust of Paul's teaching is about being careful in all we do, so that we do not hinder the Gospel. It is not just an issue of our freedom, he says, but the freedom of others. In other words, we should be careful not to do things that would cause others to stumble in their faith. The contentious verse is 1 Corinthians 11:3: *"The head of every man is Christ, the head of woman is man, and the head of Christ is God."* Later in this chapter, in verses 13-15, Paul uses phrases like "customary", "proper" and "virtuous". All of this tells us that the purpose of this passage is not to restrict women in any way, rather it is about how both men and women conduct themselves in worship. Paul is urging them to do so with appropriate cultural sensitivity, given the diverse group of people that made up the church. There were strong assumptions when it came to dress code and people were easily offended by a person's appearance. Paul urges Christians to live with consideration.

1 Corinthians 11 is not about exclusion. Verses 4-5 talk about

participation. Paul refers to *"every man who prophesies"* and *"every woman who prays or prophesies"*. Both are equally involved in public worship. The real issue here is to do with honouring or dishonouring "heads". What exactly is meant by "head" here?

On the face of it, in verse 3 it appears that Paul is teaching some kind of hierarchical order, but a closer looks shows that this is not the case. When we read the English word "head" we tend to think of "the head of an organisation" i.e. the boss, the top dog. The way the word is used here in Scripture, in its cultural context, is the key to understanding this passage. Language is never static – it evolves and changes over time. Today the word "gay" means something entirely different from what it meant to our grandparents. The word translated "head" is the Greek word *kephale*, which has a number of literal and metaphorical meanings. In this passage Paul switches between the two, sometimes meaning a literal head and sometimes a metaphorical head.

Much has been written and discussed about *kephale*. How it is understood greatly influences one's interpretation. For example, Wayne Grudem who strongly resists the role of women in the Church researched 2,336 uses of *kephale* in ancient Greek writings and chose to opt for "authority" as its meaning – even though that could only be applied to 49 of the 2,336 references, and there are 10,000 other listings in the *Thesaurus Linguae Graecae* database that he used.[1]

As an interesting side note, the only place in the New Testament where the word "authority" is used in respect of a husband and wife is 1 Corinthians 7:4, which says, *"the husband has authority over the wife's body, and the wife has authority over her husband's body"* (NASB). It is a statement that reflects mutuality in marriage. A point often missed here is that Paul backs up this point by saying specifically that *"the husband does not have authority over his own body but yields it to his wife."*

So the word *kephale* is used in many ways in ancient literature. But if Paul wanted to denote authority or a hierarchical structure, he would not have used it in this context. *Kephale* is more often used to mean "source" or "origin". If *kephale* means authority, then the logic of 1 Corinthians 11:3 puts God at the bottom of the hierarchical order! What Paul is actually teaching is an order by source, in chronological order. So then, the source of every man is Christ, as Luke writes in Acts 17:28: *"In Him we live and move and have our being."* And John begins his gospel with, *"In the beginning was the Word."* The Word brought all things into being. So, as we read in the creation narrative, the source of woman is man, just as the source of Christ is God, through the incarnation.

The context of this passage then is not about man's authority over woman. The only time authority is referred to in this passage is verse 10, which speaks about the woman's own authority. Another reason that the word translated "head" should be translated "source" is because without it, the unity of the Trinity would be distorted. Christ is not under the authority of God, the Bible teaches that Jesus is equal with God. Roger Forster has written that he is in no doubt that "source" is the meaning that the Christians at the time would have understood as they read Paul's letter, not "ruler" denoting authority.[2]

Honouring Our Source

Paul continues his letter with a discourse on head coverings. Again, the issue here is one of protocol, he is not writing about authority. At the time Jewish men wore prayer shawls and covered themselves because they felt inadequate to approach God openly. But Paul teaches in Corinthians that since the veil has been removed through Christ, we can now approach the throne of grace with boldness. In effect Paul says, "You don't need to cover your heads, as *there is now no condemnation for those who are in Christ Jesus.*" (see Romans 8:1). To tell a Jew to pray without his head covered was going against centuries of tradition, but Paul pointed out that they dishonoured their source by covering their heads when it was no longer necessary; they were free from those legalistic traditions.

Paul identifies the woman's source as man, as in creation, and says that women dishonour their source if they flaunt social conventions, projecting shame onto their male counterparts. In those days Jewish prostitutes wore long flowing hair, while Greek prostitutes had their hair cut short. As such they were easily identified in society. If Christian women followed suit, then others could read things into their appearance that might harm their reputation and impact their relationships. It seems that Christian women in Corinth were revelling in their new found freedom in Christ, and literally letting their hair down, or perhaps having it cut short. But they were doing so with no thought for long entrenched cultural norms. Hence in verse 6 Paul strongly makes the point:

"Yes, if she refuses to wear a head covering, she should cut off all her hair! But since it is shameful for a woman to have her hair cut or her head shaved, she should wear a covering."

Note that it was a disgrace then, but it's not a disgrace now. It was only a disgrace because of the culture at the time. Paul goes on to talk about "glory":

"A man ought not to cover his head for he is the image and glory of God, but the woman is the glory of man." (1 Corinthians 7)

We know from Genesis 1 that both man and woman were made in the image and glory of God. Paul is not trying to contradict what the Bible teaches elsewhere. Psalm 8 says, *"God crowned man* [both male and female] *with glory and honour.*" Paul is not denying this, he is actually raising the stakes for women. Not only is woman created in the image and glory of God, she also reflects the glory of man. She is all that man is in creation and more.

As in other places in Scripture Paul teaches equality and inter-dependency:

"In the Lord, however, woman is not independent of man, nor is man independent of woman, 'for as woman came from man, so also is man born of woman for everything comes from God.'" (v11)

The Sign of Authority

Let's return to Paul's statement in verse 10:

"For this reason, because of the angels, a woman ought to have a sign of authority on her head."

Theologian Gordon D. Fee points out that the normal way to read this Greek grammatical construction is that "the subject has the authority over the object of the preposition."[3] In other words, a woman has authority over her own head. The complementarian translation of this verse renders it "a sign of authority over her head", which adds words not in the original text and therefore changes the meaning of "authority" to "submission" to another person. The phrase "a sign of" does not appear in the original Greek. It was added by translators who were trying to make sense of the verse. It should read, "For this reason, a woman ought to have her own authority on her head." Remember that the context of this passage is not marriage. It is simply saying that the woman has her own authority on her head.

Craig Keener writes, "We should note that nothing in this passage suggests a wife's subordination. The only indicator that could be taken to mean that is the statement that man is woman's "head", but "head" in those days was capable of a variety of meanings, and nothing in this text indicates that it means subordination. As many scholars have been pointing out in the past few years, if we want this passage to teach subordination, we have to read subordination into the passage. The only clear affirmation here besides that men and women are different and should not conceal the fact, is the equality and mutual dependence of men and women."[4]

The phrase *"because of the angels"* (or *"because the angels are watching"* as the NLT has it) used by Paul in this verse is difficult to understand. There have been many bizarre interpretations that are not worth sharing here. I prefer to say that I simply don't know what this means.

Paul's letter continues with his theme of cultural convention. In verses 13-14 he writes, *"Judge for yourselves, is it proper for a woman to pray to God with her head uncovered?"* At the time, the absence of a head covering was causing a cultural blunder. Both men and women needed to be sensitive to cultural conventions. Paul's message is all about communicating Christ to others without causing offence. Reaching people for Christ is more important than us being free to do what we want to do. That is why Paul asks his readers to *"judge for yourselves"*. He is not making a doctrine that will last for all time, and Gordon Fee states that, "for Paul, it does not seem to be a life and death matter."[5]

The meaning of verse 16 is often missed due to its form of translation from Greek into English. The phrase, *"we have no other practice"* seems to imply that everywhere else women cover their heads. In fact, Paul is appealing to cultural practice and saying that he and the other churches had no custom on this, other than that the Gospel should not be hindered.

I think the summary from Grenz and Kjesbo in Women in the Church is worth quoting here:

"In the midst of the controversy surrounding the interpretation of this text in 1 Corinthians 11, what principles can we draw from the apostle's discussion? Paul obviously assumes that women, together with men, will be actively and vocally involved in public worship, specifically that they have the prerogative to pray and prophesy. The apostle's intent is not to hinder this practice, but merely to regulate the way in which men and women exercise the prerogative in the Corinthian church. There is good reason to conclude that Paul's pervasive concern for evangelism is also operative here. Believers must always act with a sense of propriety which prevents their conduct from becoming a source of offence to those outside the faith."[6]

Should Women Remain Silent?

Let us now consider the other "difficult" passage in 1 Corinthians, chapter 14 and verse 34:

"Women should remain silent in the church, as they are not allowed to speak, but must be in submission as the law says, if they want to enquire about anything they should ask their own husbands at home, for it is disgraceful for a woman to speak in the church."

Men have had a field day with this Scripture in churches. Let's examine it afresh.

First, we need to remember that this passage of Paul's letter is corrective – written to address a specific local problem. He cannot be contradicting what he wrote three chapters earlier, when he talked about women praying and prophesying in the church. He is not saying they can't do it – he has already said that they can. So the "silence" referred to here cannot be what it seems on the surface. We have already noted that there were many female leaders in the early Church who were functioning as apostles, evangelists, pastors, teachers and prophets.

Just prior to making this statement Paul has said, *"You may ALL prophesy"* (v31) – which is gender inclusive – and similarly, *"EVERYONE has a hymn"* (v26). Women were included and involved in public worship, so that is not the issue here. Read carefully in context, it is obvious that Paul is addressing a local problem. Church meetings were being disrupted – not just by women, but by men also. The Greek word translated "silent" crops up in two other places: *"If there is no interpreter, the speaker should keep* **quiet***"* (v28) and *"two or three prophets should speak and the others should weigh carefully what is said and if a revelation comes to someone who is sitting down, the first speaker should* **stop***"* (v29-30).

Throughout this passage the same Greek word is rendered "stop", "quiet" and "silent". The translators have rendered a milder English word when referring to tongue-speakers and prophets, and a stronger English word – silent – when referring to women. The word in Greek means to hush up or a voluntary silence, as God is not a God of disorder. But it is not a gagging order, otherwise it would mean that it was forbidden to laugh or cough, or make any kind of sound in church. It is not that kind of silence.

When Paul says in verse 34 that women *"should be in submission as the law says"*, this is the only place, out of the 38 times that this verb occurs in the New Testament, where the object of the submission is not clearly identified. We have to read into the text in order to arrive at the conclusion that the woman should submit to her husband. Yet nowhere in the Old Testament do we find the teaching that a woman should submit to her husband. We don't find it in the teaching of Christ either. So what law is being referred to? Remember that this passage is not about marriage but ministry. People have jumped to conclusions here, but we don't know which law Paul is referring to. Maybe it was a spiritual law, or the royal law to *"love your neighbour as yourself"* (since the flow of the passage is about being sensitive to the needs of others and not being "me-centred"). There is no conclusive answer, but we do know that there is no specific law elsewhere that says a woman should submit to a man in ministry.

Some believe Paul is referring to the Talmud, the record of rabbinic discussions pertaining to Jewish law, ethics, customs and history. Even before Christ, the traditions of the Elders had largely supplanted Moses as the principal source for conservative Jewish legal and spiritual interpretation and this extra-biblical teaching was entrenched in daily life. The Talmud silenced women and designated their speech as "shameful". Some hold the opinion that Paul is therefore referring to something that was written to him in a letter from the Corinthians when he says, *"What, did the word of God originate with you?"* (v36). His use of "what" indicates that Paul is not in agreement with whatever has been communicated to him.

Sir William Ramsey, a leading New Testament scholar, seems to agree when he writes, "We should be ready to suspect that Paul is making a quotation from the letter addressed to him by the Corinthians whenever he alludes to their knowledge, or when any statement stands in marked contrast either with the immediate context or Paul's known views."[7]

Put simply, Paul would not encourage women to speak in church in one part of his letter and then forbid them in another part of the same letter. John Temple Bristow provides some useful insight here:

"The word *phimoo* indicates a forced silence, i.e. when Jesus stilled the raging sea, quieted the unclean spirit, and silenced the Pharisees ... another word *hesuchia* is used for silence when the women were to learn in quietness – with a quiet and receptive spirit (1 Timothy 2:11-12). But in this passage, Paul uses *sigao* – a voluntary silence. It is the word used when the disciples decided to remain silent about the transfiguration (Luke 9:3-6) and when Jesus said that if the disciples were silent (*sigao*), the very stones would cry out. It is the word used for Jesus' silence during His trial (Mark 14:61) and the silence of the apostles and elders as they listened to a report by Paul and Barnabas (Acts 15:12). It's a chosen response – or it can also be a request for silence so that someone can speak (Acts 12:17). It is the kind of silence called for in the midst of disorder and tumult."[8]

Remember, there were three groups that Paul was "silencing" in this epistle: two relate to establishing correct order regarding tongues, interpretation and prophecy, and one relating to women causing disruption. The same Greek word *sigao* is used for each, which shows it is not a matter of prohibition but self-control.

What may have been happening is that women may have been ministering to others without consideration, disrupting services. Or they were trying to learn. Since women were not formally educated, and had suddenly been brought into this new life of Christian worship, often from paganism, all this was new to them. Before they had been kept at a distance from spiritual engagement, but now they were being brought it. There may have been many things they didn't understand and wanted to ask their husbands about, causing a disruption for others. Therefore Paul taught that this could not continue.

Notice Paul then says, *"If they want to enquire, let them ask at home."* This is very important, as Paul is affirming women's right to learn. It went against the culture of the day and Paul was breaking customs by commanding husbands to instruct their wives at home. They had been disadvantaged under the old system, but they must not be disadvantaged in the new community.

So the disgrace that Paul refers to is not about women ministering, it is the disgrace is disruption in public worship. He is not trying to limit or restrict women, he is addressing the chaos that prevailed in the Corinthian meetings. It was a local, cultural problem in one church. Paul was not establishing a trans-cultural law for all churches for all time. Remember that most epistles were written to individuals, people or churches. The receivers did not have the opportunity of cross referencing them with other letters, like we do with our Bibles today.

I like how The Message Bible puts these verses:

"Wives must not disrupt worship, talking when they should be listening, asking questions that could more appropriately be asked of their husbands at home. God's Book of the law guides our manners and customs here. Wives have no license to use the time of worship for unwarranted speaking. Do you—both women and men—imagine that you're a sacred oracle determining what's right and wrong? Do you think everything revolves around you? If any one of you thinks God has something for you to say or has inspired you to do something, pay close attention to what I have written. This is the way the Master wants it. If you won't play by these rules, God can't use you. Sorry."

There has to be order in church life, but this was not about silencing women as a doctrine for the Church. Rather the Church should be a community of redeemed people, where there is no class distinction, gender distinction or racial distinction.

Endnotes:

1. Grudem, Wayne, *Does Kephale Mean Source in Greek Literature?* (Trinity Journal ns 6.1 Spring 1985), p28-59.
2. Forster, Faith & Roger, *Women and the Kingdom* (PUSH Publishing, 2010), Ch7.
3. Fee, Gordon D., *God's Empowering Presence: The Holy Spirit in the Letters of*

Paul (Hendrickson, 1994), p272-81.

4. Keener, Craig S., *Paul, Women and Wives* (Hendrickson, 1992), p47.

5. Fee, Gordon D., *First Epistle to the Corinthians* (Eerdmans, 1987), p530.

6. Grenz & Kjesbo, *Women in the Church* (IVP, 1995), p115.

7. Ramsey, Sir William Mitchell, *Historical Commentary on First Corinthians* (Kregel Publications, 1996), p57.

8. Bristow, John Temple, *What Paul Really Said About Women* (HarperCollins, 1988), p62-63.

CHAPTER 8
A TALE OF TWO
CITIES: EPHESUS

We come now to the ancient stomping ground of those who seek to keep women from leadership and Christian ministry: 1 Timothy 2:8 through to 1 Timothy 3:1.

The traditional view goes something like this: Man was made first, so he has authority over woman. It was Eve who was deceived, not Adam, which shows her to be weaker and more susceptible; she caused the Fall by stepping outside her covering. Her role then, should be confined to the home and her dignity is obtained through having children. Although women are equally saved through Christ, their different roles are fixed by divine mandate.

This view is fundamentally flawed.

Bishop N.T. Wright says about this passage: "I don't think I exaggerate when I suggest that this passage above all others has been the sheet anchor for those who want to deny women a place in ordained ministry of the Church, presiding at the Eucharist, and exercising leadership within congregations."[1]

Of this passage, egalitarian Linda L. Belleville writes, "Despite a broad spectrum of biblical and extra-biblical texts that highlight female leaders, 1 Timothy 2:11–15 continues to be perceived and treated as the Great Divide in the debate."[2]

I agree. Every reader needs to appreciate that our understanding of this passage has enormous implications. Some read these verses and conclude that there is no place in today's Church for female prophets, apostles, leaders or teachers. Is that really so? If not, then we must grasp the truth and set the captives free. Let's have a look at what Paul says:

"I want men everywhere to lift up holy hands in prayer, without anger or disputing. I also want women to dress modestly, with decency and propriety, not with braided hair or gold or pearls or expensive clothes, but with good deeds, appropriate for women who profess to worship God. A woman should learn in quietness and full submission. I do not permit a woman to teach or to have authority over a man; she must be silent. For Adam was formed first, then Eve. And Adam was not the one deceived; it was the woman who was deceived and became a sinner. But women will be saved through childbearing—if they continue in faith, love and holiness with propriety. Here is a trustworthy saying 'If anyone sets his heart on being an overseer, he desires a noble task.'"

Let's first look at the background to this epistle. This letter was addressed to Timothy who was pastoring a church at Ephesus. Paul is writing to his young protégé. Paul was Timothy's mentor and father in the faith. Remember, both writer and receiver were familiar with what was being discussed, but we only see one side of the correspondence. We need to dig deeper to fully understand what is being said. In our deliberations we must consider the preponderance of Scripture. This passage in 1 Timothy is the only one in the entire Bible that appears to bar women from teaching – and it was penned by a man who had a female teacher on his team, Priscilla, who was also part of the ministry team in the church at Ephesus, of which Timothy is the pastor.

Ephesus was the fourth largest city in the Roman Empire, the

Roman capital of Asia Minor, and was located on the western coast of what we now call Turkey. Like Corinth, Ephesus was a major port attracting visitors and traders from around the world. The culture of Ephesus was predominantly Greek, so Greek influence pervaded the whole of society, though it had a large Jewish community as well. Just like Corinth, Ephesus was also a centre of cult worship. It was Aphrodite in Corinth, but Artemis in Ephesus, also known as Diana to the Romans. Bible readers are introduced to the false god Artemis in Acts 19, where there is also a record of Paul's ministry and we hear that belief in this goddess was a stronghold in that community.

The huge temple dedicated to the Artemis was built around 600BC and took 120 years to complete. It was the greatest of the Seven Wonders of the Ancient World. It also served as the largest bank in antiquity. If you arrived in Ephesus by sea it was the most prominent landmark. It was approached through 100 five-storey high marbled columns, and glistening gold of this huge idol could be seen from all around the city. Artemis was the great fertility goddess with 24 bare breasts, who was served by male eunuchs and three grades of priestesses. She was the most worshipped of all gods. In fact, in Acts 19, when Paul goes to minister there, we read in verse 27 that she was worshipped throughout Asia and the world. It is hard to imagine anything like this today. Kroeger and Kroeger wrote that, "Ephesus stood as the bastion of feminine supremacy in religion".[3]

Into this idolatrous stronghold Paul went to minister and a church was founded. He remained there for three years and had a difficult time. Eventually he was sent by the Holy Spirit to Jerusalem (Acts 20:22). He told the leaders at Ephesus, *"I don't know what awaits me, except that the Holy Spirit tells me in city after city that jail and suffering lie ahead"* (Acts 20:22-23). And

Paul would indeed write to Timothy from his prison cell.

As the church in Ephesus grew the businesses of the local silversmiths began to suffer. People were getting saved and moving away from pagan idol worship to new life in Christ. At the time of Paul's letter, the church there was 10 years old. More than a fifth of both Paul's letters to Timothy focus on addressing false teaching and heresy.

As we come to look at the content of the text in more detail, I urge readers to keep an open mind. Our faith must be strong enough to withstand fresh confrontation by Scripture. Derek and Dianne Tidball in their excellent work *The Message of Women* refer to an article in the *Guardian* newspaper which may be helpful here:

"The *Guardian* newspaper ran a couple of television advertisements. In one a skinhead initially appeared to be mugging a businessman. As the camera drew back it became apparent that far from mugging the man, the skinhead was saving him by pushing him out of the way as a pile of bricks was making its descent from above which would have almost certainly killed him. In another 'a yob' appeared to be attacking an old lady and pushing her to the ground. Again, as the camera drew back we discovered that he was in fact saving her from the path of an oncoming car. To have drawn conclusions about these young men's actions on the basis of the initial close-up pictures would have been premature and totally to misinterpret what was happening. The adverts concluded: 'it's only when you get the whole picture you can fully understand what's going on'. A narrow focus can sometimes lead to misinterpretation."[4]

This is certainly true when we look at this passage. Bearing in mind its importance, we are going to look at nine things about women, going through it verse by verse, keeping in mind the context and the culture outlined above.

1. Women and Dress

"I also want women to dress modestly, with decency and propriety, not with braided hair or gold or pearls or expensive clothes." (2 Timothy 2:9)

A gender and sexual revolution was taking place in many of the major cities of the Roman Empire which resulted in women expressing their new found freedom by flouting even the norms of the Romans. Caesar Augustus passed laws legislating what respectable women were to wear and how prostitutes and adulteresses were to dress. Naturally, people were not complying.

Not many readers will have heard a sermon on "Thou Shalt Not Wear Pearls", yet in this passage that is what Paul says he wants. Have you ever heard a sermon saying you should not wear expensive clothes? We ignore such statements as culturally irrelevant, then try to apply a verse like, *"women should learn in quietness and full submission."* It's not right for us to pick and choose, interpreting one statement contextually and making another a rule for all time.

The point of verse 9 is connected to the previous verse in which Paul says that he wants men to pray without having anger and to stop disputing. So there was an issue amongst the men that needed addressing and, in addition, the women were to stop flaunting themselves. To the Romans, pearls were the greatest of jewels, so to wear them was considered to be a display of vanity. If women were drawing attention to themselves by displaying their wealth like this – which could be misconstrued as being sexually promiscuous – then the Gospel could be hindered. As Bruce Winter writes, "the public perception of Christian wives was a critical matter in the community … they could play into the hands of the enemy of the early Christian movement in Ephesus if they dressed like high-class prostitutes."[5]

Removing any hindrance to spreading the Gospel was always at the top of Paul's agenda, so he addresses the heart of the issue. In verse 10 he pleads for women to make themselves attractive by their good deeds. In other words, if you profess to worship God, do so modestly. Nothing should hinder the Gospel, especially not through wealthy members of the church looking very glamorous when there were perhaps poor people also in attendance. It is not really clothes or jewels that Paul is concerned with, but attitudes.

2. Women and Learning

In verse 11 Paul goes on to say, *"A woman should **learn** in quietness and submission."* We have already highlighted the revolutionary nature of this statement. Allowing women to study required a paradigm shift in Jewish and Greek thinking. In fact, in the original text the word translated "should" is much stronger. It really says women must learn or be taught the word of God. The "quietness and submission" then is not a muzzling of women, it refers to an attitude of learning. Paul is saying that women *must* be taught and should learn with a proper attitude. The Greek word here is *esuchia* which means "peaceful or quiet, a listening attitude, paying studious attention". The meaning of "submission" in this context is the exact opposite of being self-centred or grasping. Women were not used to being in a learning environment, so they needed some instruction on how to learn. Can you imagine going into a place like Afghanistan, where women are treated badly by the Taliban, and trying to teach those women without actually showing them how they learn?

Paul says that women must learn, and they should do so with a proper spirit – a humble attitude. This would be the same for anyone, including men. It is hard to teach anyone who keeps butting in or is not open to instruction, and that is what is being addressed here.

3. Women and Teaching

As we arrive at Verse 12 we remember that women exercised teaching roles in the early Church. Priscilla taught theology to Apollos. Paul tells Timothy to greet her, not to stop her! In 2 Timothy 4:19 Paul is obviously not contradicting himself, so these verses demand careful study.

"I do not permit a woman to teach or to have authority over a man; she must be silent." (v12)

Superficially, in English, the sentence appears to be very clear indeed, but it is not so clear in the Greek. The key to understanding this verse hinges on the Greek verb *authentia* which is rendered here as "authority". Once again we see that this word is used only once, here, in the whole New Testament. Apart from in this verse it is not used much in other ancient literature around this time.

Before we go further, let's remind ourselves of the absurdity of the flat book approach. Taken at face value it would mean that a woman could never teach anything, anywhere. It would also make it a sin for a man to ever listen to and learn from a woman. In fact, women should not talk at all! There could be no female Sunday School teachers, no lecturers etc. Some may argue that it only pertains to church life, but that assumption could not be based on what Paul actually said. Even those against egalitarianism agree that this verse has to be interpreted. We are, however, prone to interpret them according to our own biases and traditions. Faithfulness to the word of God demands that we interpret it in the light of the rest of Scripture.

In his letters to Timothy, Paul reminds him of the teaching he received from two godly women, his relatives. Paul does not try to correct this. He has nothing against women teaching. We have already learnt how women in Corinth were prophesying with Paul's encouragement. Priscilla taught with Paul's blessing and she was a great Bible teacher. The Word "prophesying" in 1 Corinthians 14:26 is described as a "word of instruction". Thus women were giving words of instruction in the church in Corinth. Neither is this a problem for Paul. Obviously then Paul is not saying that women cannot speak in church, and it cannot mean that women should not teach. What we have in Ephesus is a particular situation. The issue being addressed here is *false teaching.*

In 2 Timothy 2:2 Paul writes, *"the things you have heard me say in the presence of many witnesses entrust to reliable men who will also be qualified to teach others."* Those who oppose women in leadership/ministry have often referred to Paul's use of the word "men", but that is just the English translation. The Greek word *anthrōpous* is gender inclusive, meaning "people", male and female. If Paul had wanted to stipulate that only men should teach he would have used the word *andros* meaning men, but he did not. This is the same gender-inclusive word used in 1 Timothy 2:4: *"...who wants all **men** [people] to be saved and to come to a knowledge of the truth."* 1 Timothy 2:8 does use the word andros – *"I want men everywhere to lift up holy hands in prayer, without anger or disputing"* – but that is because Paul is first making a point about men, followed by a point about women.

Moving back to verse 12 – *"I do not permit a woman to teach"* – we see that there is no imperative command in this verse. Rather it is written in the present tense and actually means, "I do not permit a woman to teach now" or "I am not permitting...". It is not a rule for all time. So what was the false teaching Paul was addressing?

The church had a particular problem with women who were spreading a false teaching linked to Gnosticism. In fact, because the pronouns change from plural to singular, it could also be that there was a *particular* woman in the church who was being a bad influence (some commentators and translators suggest this). It is interesting that in this letter Paul writes a lot about widows, younger widows, and about old wives tales, which were inbred into the culture. This false teaching was a major problem to the church and it seems that it was coming mainly from a women or a specific woman. If you look back at 1 Timothy 1:3, Paul also commands certain men not to teach as well. There was a real problem with false doctrine spreading through the community and affecting the life of the church.

As Graham Cole writes in his book, *Women Teaching Men the Bible: What's The Problem?*: "It should be honestly acknowledged that many men have assumed positions of teaching authority who are far less able, gifted or informed than women, to the detriment of the Church. One's authority to teach is not a matter of gender but of one's ability to faithfully explain and apply God's word to a congregation."[6]

The summary of F.F. Bruce on this passage is, "this was a particular instruction for a local problem."[7]

I remember some years ago listening to Dr Gilbert Bilezekien teaching a class in Willow Creek Church, Chicago. The point he made about this passage was that it was a corrective passage for a particular situation during a specific time, and not a teaching passage similar to that in the book of Romans. For that reason, Paul did not ask for this letter to be copied and sent to other churches, as he did with the letter to the Colossians (Colossians 4:16), for instance. So to try and build an everlasting practice from a letter of correction would be as dangerous as building a doctrine based on a parable.

We see a similar thing in Acts chapter 15, for example. Gentiles were to be included in the new community without first becoming Jews. However, to accommodate the cultural sensitivities of believing Jews, the Gentiles were instructed not to eat blood or animals killed by strangulation. Over time, how an animal was killed or whether a person ate his steak rare ceased to become an instrument of division. The meat issue was a temporary concession to cultural sensitivities.

Similarly, Paul's prohibition was never intended as a fixed principle for all time, but a wise prohibition in a specific circumstance that needs to be applied in all situations where such circumstances are repeated. There are many enthusiastic people today, for instance, who set themselves up as teachers and leaders, but don't have the required character or gifting and need to be restrained. This applies to both men and women.

The fact that Paul is talking about women learning is a clue here. Learning precedes teaching. Anyone teaching without learning will end up teaching error. So Paul is saying that women should not be teaching until they have been trained in the Scriptures. Hence the command, "Don't teach at the moment" or "I don't want that woman, or women, teaching until they have learned."

Esteemed Bible teacher J.I. Packer writes,

"I think it is an open question whether in our day Paul would have forbidden a woman to teach from the Bible. It is an open question whether he would have regarded what happened to Eve in the Garden of Eden as sufficient reason for forbidding a woman to teach from the Bible. When you teach from the Bible, in any situation at all, what you are saying to people is, 'Look, I am trying to tell you what it says. I speak as to wise men and women. You have your Bibles. You follow along. You judge what I say.' No claim to personal authority with regard to the substance of the message is being made at all. It seems to me that this significant difference between teaching then and teaching now does, in fact, mean that the prohibition on women preaching and teaching need not apply."[8]

Philip B. Payne agrees, as he writes in his brilliant work *Man and Woman, One in Christ*, "First Timothy 2:12 does not support a universal prohibition of women teaching or having authority over men. Nothing in this passage states that women are inherently unsuited to teach or exercise authority over men in spiritual or any other matters. Nor does Paul universalize this particular prohibition for all churches and all times."[9]

Having said this, Paul now moves on to "…or to have authority over a man" which we will now consider.

4. Women and Authority

This fragment of a verse has historically been used to build fundamental church practice, when in actual fact it only addresses a specific church problem. Many have assumed that women cannot be church leaders, which is a big mistake for two reasons: First, because the issue is not about leadership and secondly because church leadership in the way that Christ taught it, and the way it is taught in the New Testament, is not about *anybody* having authority over *anyone*. We need to understand true spiritual authority. The Bible is very clear that no one is to wield this kind of authority over anyone else, be it male over female or vice-versa.

We have mentioned that the Greek verb *authentia* (translated "authority") only appears in this one place. The word Paul usually uses for authority is *exousia*. This in itself make is precarious to deny women on the uncertain meaning of a verb that occurs nowhere else in the Bible. But it is even more precarious to assume that the meaning is to have authority.

If Paul had wanted to speak of the ordinary exercise of authority he could have picked any number of words, but he used *exousia* 26 times in 7 different letters. Since he did not use it here, we must ask why. There must be something about the word *authentia* that particularly fits the Ephesian situation. Here, "authority" describes the worst possible form of domination and manipulation.

Throughout the history of Greek literature, particularly from 200 BC to 200 AD, *authentein* represented something notoriously violent. Leland Wilshire documents this in his book entitled, *Insight into Two Biblical Passages: The Anatomy of a Prohibition, 1 Timothy 2:12, the TLG Computer, and the Christian Church*. According to Wilshire, *authentein* had the following meanings:

- "doer of a massacre
- author of crimes
- perpetrators of sacrilege
- supporter of violent actions
- murderer of oneself
- perpetrator of slaughter
- murderer
- slayer
- slayer of oneself
- authority
- perpetrator of evil
- one who murders by his own hand."[10]

Linda Belleville in her book, *Discovering Biblical Equality* shows from her studies that authentein means to "dominate", rather than "to exercise authority over". Rosie Ward supports these findings when she writes, "there is no lexical warrant for translating the word 'to exercise authority over', this meaning did not appear until several centuries later."[11]

The cult of Artemis, the false fertility goddess, taught that women were superior to men and practiced and taught dominance of women over men. From that false teaching there was a stream of gnostic heresy that was magnifying the role of women, building Eve up above Adam, thus dishonouring men. This stream of false teaching was creeping into the Church, therefore Paul counteracts it. Of course, this kind of domineering, manipulating or controlling behaviour would be condemned by the Bible for both genders.

5. Women and Creation

Now we come to 1 Timothy 2:13: *"For Adam was formed first, then Eve."* Many people have used this little phrase to teach that men are superior to women, but this argument holds no weight. There was no such hierarchy before the Fall and nothing to indicate that woman was inferior to man or vice versa. In addition, nowhere else in the New Testament does the term "first" mean "superior". It always refers to a sequence e.g. in 1 Thessalonians 4:16: *"the dead in Christ shall rise first."* This does not indicate superiority, it is just about sequence. The fact that John the Baptist came first does not make Jesus inferior to John. Paul is simply quoting a biblical fact. Even John Calvin, who suppressed women's ministry, admitted that the argument about woman being created second, "appears not to be a very strong argument in favour of her subjection."[12]

There was no hierarchy before the Fall where man and woman dwelt in unity and equality. It was only after the Fall, as a result of sin, that conflict arose. However, the Bible teaches that the cross cancels and reverses those consequences. Why then does Paul even need to mention it? Because his purpose is to counteract the heresy of the false teaching spread by the Gnostics that Eve was the originator and source of Adam's life.

In the pagan religious culture of Ephesus, some taught that life had its origin in Cybele, a woman, and that sin originated with various male gods, including Cybele's unfaithful consort, Attis. Women were seen as virtuous and men as evil. It is difficult for us today to fully grasp the endless myths, legends and superstitions that permeated society at that time. Cybele was known as the mother of all gods and as the parent of human beings and beasts. Her priests, known as the Galli, castrated themselves on entering her service, which was justified on the basis that her lover Attis had emasculated himself under a pine tree where he bled to death. This was commemorated annually in March at her shrine.

There was also teaching that the serpent was a greater deity than God and that Eve was Adam's instructor. In fact, in the previous chapter, 1 Timothy 1:4, the apostle writes about people who are *"devoting themselves to myths and endless genealogies"*, which was part of the problem of the day. Much of the error and false doctrine revolved around the positioning of men and women. So Paul is correcting and counteracting false doctrine by saying Eve was not made first. He was not, however, trying to make a law against all women for all time.

Philip Payne writes, "In no other verse of Scripture is it stated that women are not to be in authority over men. It is precarious indeed to deny that women should ever be in a position of authority over men based on the disputed meaning of the only occurrence of this word anywhere in the Bible."[13]

6. Women and Deception
In 1 Timothy 2:14, Paul writes, *"...and Adam was not the one deceived, it was the woman who was deceived and became a sinner."*

A superficial reading of this text makes it sound as though

Adam was innocent and Eve the guilty one; that she was the sinner, not him. However, we know from other Scripture that that is not true. Again Paul was simply declaring biblical truth to expose the local error. Some Gnostics taught that Eve bore no blame in the Fall whatsoever. In fact the Gnostics said that humanity took a great step forward, as Eve sought to grab this knowledge. Paul draws an analogy here between the woman deceived in the garden and the woman/women being deceived in Ephesus. It is exactly the same thing that he wrote in Corinthians. In 2 Corinthians 11:3, Paul says, *"I am afraid that just as Eve was deceived by the serpent's cunning, your minds may somehow be led astray."* To the Corinthians he was talking to both men and women. Here was a different church, a different picture, a different culture. Paul is now saying that, just as Eve was deceived, so some specific woman/women are in deception right now.

People have built a completely fallacious doctrine out of Paul's words that women are more easily deceived that men. Mark Driscoll obviously supports this error with his statement, "Paul is simply stating that when it comes to leading in the church, women are unfit because they are more gullible and easier to deceive than men."[14]

It is hardly surprising that Mark Driscoll and others have made such a huge mistake, given the negative and misogynistic vitriol that has come from the Church Fathers of the past:

Augustine (354-430):

"And (Satan) first tried his deceit upon the woman, making his assault upon *the weaker part of that human alliance,* that he might gradually gain the whole, and *not supposing that the man would readily give ear to him, or be deceived,* but that he might yield to the error of the woman … For not without significance did the apostle say, 'and Adam was not deceived, but the woman being deceived was in the transgression.'"[15]

Epiphanius (365-403):

"The female sex is easily mistaken, fallible and poor in intelligence. It is apparent that through women the devil has vomited this forth … come now servants of God, let us *put on a manly mind* and disperse the mania of these women. The whole of this deception is female: the disease comes from Eve who was long ago deceived."[16]

Bonaventure (1217-1274):

"The devil, envious of man, assumed the form of a serpent and addressed the woman … By this temptation, he sought to bring about the fall of *the weaker woman, so that through her he might then overthrow the stronger sex…*"[17]

Thomas Aquinas (1225-1274):

"The human group would have lacked the benefit of order had some of its members not been governed by others *who were wiser.* Such is the subjection in which woman is by nature subordinate to man, because *the power of rational discernment is by nature stronger in man.*"[18]

Erasmus (1466-1536):

"Eve was deceived first when, believing the serpent and beguiled by the enticement of the fruit, she disregarded God's command. The man *could not have been taken in* by the serpent's promises or by the allure of the fruit: only the love for his wife drew him into a ruinous compliance!"[19]

Martin Luther (1483-1536):

"Paul thus has proved that by divine and human right that Adam is the master of the woman. That is, it was not Adam who went astray. Therefore, *there was greater wisdom in Adam than in the woman* ... Adam persevered in his dominion over the serpent, which did not attack him, but rather attacked the weaker vessel just as he does today!"[20]

John Knox (1514-1572):

"And first, where that I affirm the empire of a woman to be a thing repugnant to nature, I mean not only that God by the order of creation has spoiled woman of authority and dominion, but also that man has seen, proved and pronounced just causes what that it should be so ... *for who can deny but it is repugnant to nature, that the blind shall be appointed to lead and conduct such as do see? That the weak, the sick and impotent persons shall nourish and keep the whole and strong, and finally, that the foolish and frantic shall govern the discreet. And give counsel to such as be of sober mind? And such be all women, compared to man in bearing authority* ... Nature I say, does pain them further to be weak, frail, impatient, feeble and foolish; and experience has declared them to be inconstant, variable, cruel and lacking the spirit of counsel and regiment."[21]

John Gill (1697-1771):

"Now inasmuch as the serpent did not attack Adam, he being *the stronger and more knowing person* and less capable of being managed and seduced; but made his attempt on Eve, in which he succeeded; and since not Adam, but Eve, was deceived, it appears that man is the more proper person to bear rule and authority, as in civil and domestic, so in ecclesiastical affairs; and it is right for the woman to learn and the men to teach."[22]

Henry P. Liddon (1829-1890):

"The point is that Eve's *facility in yielding to the deceiver* warrants the Apostolic rule which forbids a woman to teach … the experience of all ages that *woman is more easily led away than man*, is warranted by what is said of the first representative of the sex."[23]

These are just a few examples of historical theological influence that have negatively influenced the Church in its thinking about women.

In other words, many Christians have been taught that what caused the Fall was the fact that the woman stepped out of line when she should have stayed under her husband's "headship". The point that is missed is that before the Fall there was no headship of man over woman – they both had equal dominion; both ruled; it was a shared partnership with God.

So there was no role-reversal or hierarchy, the issue is deception. If Eve's teaching was defective, guess who taught her? Adam received the revelation from God about what trees to touch and not to touch before Eve was made. She received the knowledge from Adam. Guess who stood alongside her when the tempter came and who never said a word? Guess who took a bite without any resistance when his wife gave it to him? And guess whose name was on the lips of God when He came looking? It was the man, Adam. So if the woman was deceived, the man was disobedient.

When the woman was challenged by God, *"What have you done?"* she said, *"the serpent deceived me."* When the man was challenged by God, *"What have you done?"* he said *"The woman YOU gave me…"*. It is a grave error to make the woman the sinner and not the man. Elsewhere Paul makes it very clear that it was Adam's sin, not Eve's sin, that brought sin, death and condemnation into our world.

As Derek and Dianne Tidball point out, "For the most part, Paul attributes the fall of humanity to Adam, explaining typically, 'just as sin entered the world through one man bringing death to all, so by God's grace, justification, righteousness and eternal life is made possible through 'the one man Jesus Christ.' (Romans 5:12, 16-17, 19; 1 Corinthians 15:22). Paul's attribution of "blame" to Eve occurs on only one occasion (1 Timothy 2:14) and is heavily outweighed by the responsibility he puts on Adams shoulders."[24]

So Paul is simply declaring to the false teachers who denied Eve had any part in the Fall, she was deceived. The Gnostics said she bore no guilt. "Wrong," says Paul. He is correcting a local issue. It is a disgrace that this verse has been twisted to shackle so many gifted women. Many in depth studies have proven that, in fact, susceptibility to deception has to do with age, experience, intelligence, education and personality – it is nothing to do with gender!

In the 19th Century, black people were denied an education. Clarissa C. Lawrence, a black Vice President of the Salem Female Anti-Slavery Society, said in 1838, "Faith and prayer will do wonders in the Anti-Slavery cause, place yourselves dear friends in our stead. We are blamed for not filling useful places in society, but give us light, give us learning, and see then what places we can occupy."[25]

The same cry rises up from women all around the world: "Unshackle us and see what we can do!"

7. Women and Childbirth

1 Timothy 2:15 reads, *"but women will be saved through*

childbearing." This meaning of this verse is not easy to fathom and has stretched the minds of many. The main views and opinions of scholars are these:

1. A woman would be saved through child-bearing ultimately by bringing the Messiah into the world, the seed of the woman.
2. She would be saved by accepting a subordinate role and being domesticated at home.
3. She would be saved from death during labour, which would mean that no Christian would ever die in childbirth, which sadly has not been the case.

So what is the *real* meaning? If you were pregnant in Ephesus at the time when Paul wrote this, you had a 50/50 chance of dying during childbirth. Giving birth was a dangerous thing. Artemis, goddess of fertility, was worshipped widely, and it was believed that if you made an offering to her during pregnancy, you would be protected in childbirth. So this great centre of cultish religious worship said, "Bring an offering to Artemis and she will save you." In response Paul said, "By the way, you will be saved in childbirth, but not through Artemis!" In other words, put your trust in God and be committed to Him. Paul does not mention or defame Artemis, and there was great wisdom in that. Paul had a history in Ephesus. When people were getting saved, others were saying that Paul was robbing them of their trade. Paul was shrewd not to blaspheme their goddess, but nevertheless he corrects the theological error.

8. Women and Eldership

In 1 Timothy 3:1, bearing in mind there were no chapter divisions in the original text, Paul says, *"If anyone sets his heart on being an overseer, he desires a noble task."* Some translations render "anyone" as "he", but in the Greek it is gender-inclusive, not specifically male. The opening sentence of 1 Timothy chapter 3 literally says, "...If someone aspires to overseer-ship, he/she desires a fine task." There is no gender preference suggested here.

As Phillip Payne points out, "Unfortunately, practically all English versions of 1 Timothy 3:1-13 and Titus 1:5-9 give the false impression that Paul uses masculine pronouns, implying that these church leaders must be male. In the Greek, however, there is not even one masculine pronoun or 'men only' requirement for the office of overseer and deacon."[26]

An example of the misleading nature of some translations is The New Living Translation (NLT), which has taken the bold step of inserting the statement, *"So an elder must be a man..."* in 1 Timothy 3:2. This statement simply does not appear anywhere in any Greek manuscript of the New Testament. The translators of the NLT have inserted this statement to express their opinion that a church leader must be a man. Had Paul wanted to say, "An elder (or overseer) must be a man" he would have clearly done so.

Although in the Scriptures there are no women mentioned by name as elders, there are only two men mentioned by name and surprisingly the only deacon mentioned by name is a woman, Phoebe. But as the Bible speaks elsewhere of women deacons, women apostles, women teachers and women prophets, there is no reason at all why women should not be elders. Nowhere does Paul ever try to restrict gifted, godly women from leadership roles in the New Testament.

Within the qualification list for elders there is only one reference that is exclusively masculine, that is, *"the elder must be the husband of one wife"* or literally, "a one woman man". Fundamentally Paul is teaching marital faithfulness and ruling out bigamy and infidelity. There was no need to say the same about women as women scarcely had two husbands! Neither does this verse prohibit single people who were not married and unable to have *"children that believe"*. Otherwise Paul, probably Barnabas and Timothy, and definitely Jesus are all excluded. To use this passage to exclude women would mean, for the sake of honesty and consistency, that unmarried, childless people, or those with just one child, should also be excluded, which would conflict with Scriptures like 1 Corinthians 7:25-35 which supports it.

In Titus 1:5-2:5, Paul uses the Greek word *presbytas* for male elders and *presbytidas* for women elders – a similar word to *presbytera* in 1 Timothy 5:2. This word *presbytidas* refers to women leaders, which is evidenced by many examples of women's names on tombstones in the second and third centuries, called *presbyteras*. Qualifications are laid down for both, but in no way were the women treated like second-class citizens.

A similar thing happens in Romans 12:8 where the NIV version says, *"If it is leadership, let him govern diligently"* which infers that leadership is male. However, the NIV has added eight masculine pronouns where none occur in the Greek. There is no passage in the New Testament using this verb "to rule" that excludes women. In fact, the only New Testament use of the noun form of this verb describes a woman, Phoebe, in Romans 16:2.

Proponents of male-only ministry interpret 1 Timothy 3:11 as meaning deacons' wives, in an attempt to avoid accepting the fact that women could be and were deacons in the first century Church, but an unbiased reading makes it pretty conclusive that it is female deacons that are being referred to. In the light of Phoebe being referred to as a deacon there is no reason to distort the obvious meaning here. At the time that this letter was written, both men and women were referred to as deacons. Historians Kevin Madigan and Carolyn Osiek cite 61 inscriptions and forty literary references to female deacons through the sixth century AD, in the East where the church in Ephesus was located.[27]

Martin Scott says that, "Although it is true that given the culture most elders were male, the text itself does not rule out the possibility of women elders, unless women are specifically restricted, we should seek to include them."[28]

The question we should ask is, "Where in the New Testament is a woman directly prohibited from being an elder?"

Writing in *Hidden History of Women Leaders in the Church* Maria Boccia reveals how women were in leadership positions up until the 3rd and 4th centuries and states:

"Women were systematically excluded by decrees of church councils, actions of bishops and popes and sociocultural pressures. This meant that they were no longer allowed to function in offices they had held in earlier centuries. The historical evidence shows that women were elders up until the Synod of Laodicea in the fourth century but then during the 4th and 5th century, the Christian church gradually extinguished women's access to positions of power in the church. At the Council of Laodicea (352 AD), women were forbidden from the priesthood. They also were prohibited from presiding over churches. They decided that 'One ought not to establish in the church the women called overseers (*presbytidas*) … women must not approach the altar."[29]

At the Fourth Synod of Carthage (398 AD) it was declared, "A woman however learned and holy, may not presume to teach men in an assembly … A woman may not baptise."[30]

At the Council of Chalcedon (451 AD), Canon #15 of the Council states, "No woman under 40 years of age is to be ordained a deacon, and then only after close scrutiny."[31]

In summary, I echo the words of Simon Ponsonby, Dean of Studies at the Oxford Centre for Church Growth and theologian at St Aldates Church, Oxford, who writes:

"The texts that appear to prohibit women from senior church leadership roles are the very same ones that appear to prohibit women from preaching or teaching men in any capacity. Consequently, I see only two possible positions: all or nothing. Either the passages in 1 Corinthians 12 and 1 Timothy 2 do permanently prohibit women from leading and preaching roles and the matter is closed ... or those texts are not rightly understood or applied as comprehensive prohibitions and other texts such as Romans 16 that appear to legitimate women's ministries must take priority. If that is the case, then no offices are excluded to women, who may exercise all ministries in the church if they exhibit the Spirit's charisms and character to do so. Paul's practice of recognising and releasing, praising and partnering with women leaders, must inform how we interpret and apply other texts. If that was Paul's practice, it must become ours. Women's gifts must be identified, honoured, nurtured and released, without imposing a stained-glass ceiling. Not to do so is to dishonour the gift-giving Sprit, to disempower women made in God's image, to diminish the nature of church, and to damage God's action for the world."[32]

If one understands the New Testament correctly the clear conclusion is that it is *gifting* not *gender* that determines ministry and leadership.

Before moving on, I will let one of the world's leading Bible Scholars, N.T. Wright, sum up the issue with this passage:

"I believe we have seriously misread the relevant passages in the New Testament, not least through a long process of assumption, tradition, and all kinds of post-biblical and sub-biblical attitudes that have crept into Christianity. Just as I think we need to radically change our traditional pictures of the afterlife, away from medieval models and back to biblical ones, so we need to radically change our traditional pictures of what men and women are and of how they relate to one another within the church, and indeed of what the Bible says on this subject. I do wonder sometimes, if those who present radical challenges to Christianity have not been all the more eager to make out that the Bible says certain things about women as an excuse for claiming that Christianity in general is a wicked thing that should be abandoned. Of course, plenty of Christians have given outsiders enough chances to make that sort of comment. But perhaps in our generation we have an opportunity to take a large step back in the right direction."[33]

I am in complete agreement with his statement.

9. Women and Submission

Writing in Ephesians 5:22-23 Paul says, *"Wives, submit to your husbands as to the Lord. For the husband is the head of the wife as Christ is the head of the church."* This verse, or rather part of it, has often been quoted out of context, usually ignoring the verse that precedes it: *"submit to one another out of reverence for Christ."* The two verses are actually one sentence in the original Greek, so in fact Paul is calling for mutual submission.

In the wives section of the sentence there is no verb in the Greek. It literally reads, *"wives to your husbands as to the Lord."* You have to find the verb in the previous section, about submitting to one another. Paul cleverly ensures that his words can't be misquoted. We have to include the bit about mutual submission to make sense of the bit about marriage.

There are 328 Greek words here that contain eight direct commands, five of the commands are addressed to MEN, two are addressed to CHILDREN, one to SLAVES, and NONE TO WOMEN. There are 40 words that address the wife's role, 150 words that address the husband's role, 35 to children, 59 to slaves and 28 to masters. In this passage that is so often used to put women in their place, the thrust of the teaching is aimed at men!

In the ancient world, they had what was known as the "Household Code" – a socially accepted household management guide that established a pattern for family life. It stated that the husband was in charge of his wife, fathers over their children, masters over their slaves. This code had existed for hundreds of years and was mirrored in the Church. Mention of it appears in 1 Peter 3:1-9; Ephesians 5:21-33 and Colossians 3:18-19. New Testament writers generally encouraged the new believers to continue following the code to ensure that nothing hindered the spread of the Gospel or brought it into disrepute.

Nevertheless, the thrust of Paul's teaching always underlines the mutuality of submission. In chapter 6 of Ephesians he calls for something that people were unfamiliar with – that no one had thought of before, especially given the acceptance of the household code. He says, *"Fathers, **do not** exasperate your children."* This was a radical departure from accepted thinking. Paul was saying that respect and submission is a two-way street. It's mutual; it doesn't just work one way. He goes on to tell the Ephesians that they are ALL heirs: male, female, bond, free, Jew, Gentile.

In the second half of our opening Scripture quote, verse 23 of Ephesians 5, we have this word "head" again: *"For the husband is the head of the wife as Christ is the head of the church."* Dr Gilbert Bilezikian says in his book *Beyond Sex Roles* that, "The use of 'head' within the context where it is found in 1 Corinthians, Ephesians and Colossians forces on us the conclusion that the concept of 'headship' in the New Testament refers to the function of Christ as the fountainhead of life and growth, and to His servant role as provider and sustainer." He goes on to point out that the term "head" in relation to Christ is used five times in Scripture to define the relationship of Christ to the Church (Ephesians 1:22-23; 4:15-16; 5:23; Colossians 1:18-19; 2;19) and is never used in an authority role.[34]

The New Testament contains no text where Christ's headship to the Church connotes a relationship of authority and likewise the New Testament contains no text where a husband's headship to his wife connotes a relationship of authority. The word actually means "source, sustainer and nourisher".

Colin Brown writes in the Dictionary of New Testament Theology, "The headship and lordship of Christ does not consist in authoritarianism. Rather it is expressed precisely in self-giving. Likewise, the husband's headship is to be exercised in the same self-giving in which he lives out his new nature in Christ. The headship consists in a renunciation of all authoritarianism; the only subjection that it is to demand is self-subjection for love of the wife."[35]

The Gospel sowed seeds of social change that would radically affect what once permeated the whole of the society into which it was being preached. Paul challenged the behaviour of all. The summary of the teaching in verse 22 is at the end, in verse 33. *"Each one of you must love his wife as he loves himself, and the wife must respect her husband."* When you love someone sacrificially, you are submitted to them. When Paul said to the men to love their wives as they loved themselves, that was totally radical. It raised the status of women, rather than put them down.

Tony Campolo tells the story of a pastor who had a woman come to him who was being beaten by her husband. The pastor told her to go home and be in submission to her husband, who was the head of her house. She went home and the husband killed her. The family challenged the pastor, "Why on earth did you send our loved one back to that monster?" The pastor said he was just doing what the Bible told him to do! That is not true. Nowhere does it teach that a woman has to be in submission to a monster like that. Nowhere. The idea of anybody lording it over somebody in the home, or in church, is absent from Scripture. Any authority is a "servant-authority".

It's important to note too that just because a man is told to love his wife, that doesn't exclude the wife from loving her husband; and just as the wife is told to submit to her husband, that doesn't exclude the husband from submitting to his wife. The text says *"submit to one another out of reverence for Christ."*

Lawrence Richardson in the *Word Bible Handbook* says, "Like many other Bible terms, the concept of 'headship' has been warped by importing secular notions. To call someone head of a corporation or project identifies him as a person with control over others, but the New Testament term is not used in this sense. Instead, the biblical emphasis of 'head' is 'source' or 'origin', thus Jesus as 'head' over everything for the Church is seen as 'source and sustainer of life of His body'. Headship does not speak of power but of serving."[36]

One aspect of the mutual submission taught in verse 21 is that the word "obey" does not appear in Scripture with respect to wives, though it does with respect to children and slaves (Ephesians 6:1; 6:5). The analogy between the relationship of Christ to the Church and that of the husband to the wife is basic to the entire passage. Verse 25 says, *"Husbands love your wives just as Christ loved the church and gave himself up for her."* Paul shows that this is not a one-sided submission, but a reciprocal relationship. It is an expression of how the husband ought to devote himself to his wife's good. To give oneself up to death for his beloved is a more extreme expression of devotion for the man than the wife is called on to make for her husband.

When Paul writes chapter 6 he moves to the issue of slaves obeying their masters. Professor Craig S. Keener from Duke University says this: "Modern writers who argue that Paul's charge to wives is to submit to their husbands as to Christ and is binding in all cultures, must come to grips with the fact that Paul more plainly tells slaves to obey their masters as they would Christ. If one is binding in all cultures so is the other! We have abolished slavery thankfully, even though the scripture says slaves obey your masters."[37]

So why was Paul saying that? He was saying that this cultural mind-set would not get changed overnight. Cultural change takes time. As the power of the Gospel touches and changes people's hearts and lives, cultural transformation begins to occur, but in the meantime, Christians must live in ways that will complement and not hinder the Gospel.

The Church has failed women. Heaven has been calling the Church for the last 2,000 years to set women free to do what God has called, created and wired them to do, but largely the Church has been slow and resistant to hear.

Endnotes:

1. Wright N.T., *Surprised by Scripture* (HarperCollins, 2014), p78.

2. Pierce & Groothius, *Discovering Biblical Authority* (IVP, 2004), p205.

3. Kroeger & Kroeger, *I Suffer Not a Woman* (Baker, 2012), p54.

4. Tidball, Derek & Dianne, *The Message of Women* (IVP, 2012), p256.

5. Winter, Bruce, W., *Roman Wives* (Eerdmans, 2003), p121.

6 Cole, Graham, *Women Teaching Men the Bible* (Zadok Perspectives, 2007), p95.

7. Tidball, Derek & Dianne, *The Message of Women*. Quoting from Nashville Conference in 1988, pp11-15.

8. *The Proceedings of the Conference on Biblical Interpretation*, Nashville, 1988, pp11-15.

9. Payne, Philip B., *Man and Woman, One in Christ* (Zondervan, 2009), p444.

10. Wilshire, Leland E., *Insight Into Two Biblical Passages: The Anatomy of a Prohibition*, 1 Timothy 2:12, the TLG Computer, and the Christian Church. (University Press of America, 2010), p22.

11. Ward, Rosie, *Growing Women Leaders* (BRF, 2008), p29.

12. Calvin, John, *Commentary on Timothy, Titus & Philemon* (Wipf & Stock Publishers, 2006), p68.

13. Payne, Philip, *Man and Woman, One in Christ* (Zondervan, 2009), p397.

14. Sark, Thom, *The Human Faces of God* (Wipf & Stock Publishers, 2011), p16.

15. Augustine, *The City of God*, pp458-459.

16. Webb, William J., *Slaves, Women & Homosexuals* (IVP, 2001), p264.

17. Tucker, Ruth A., *Women in the Maze* (InterVarsity Press, 1992), p165.

18. Thomas Aquinas, *Man Made in the Image of God* (McGraw Hill, 1963-1974), p13;37-39.

19. Sider, Robert D., *The Collected Works of Erasmus* (University of Toronto Press, 1993), p17.

20. Martin Luther, *Lectures on 1 Timothy in Luther's Works* (Concordia, 1973), p28;278-279.

21. Knox, John, *The First Blast of the Trumpet Against the Monstrous Regiment of Women* (AMS reprint, 1967), p11-12.

22. Webb, William T., *Slaves, Women & Homosexuals* (InterVarsity Press, 2001), p266.

23. Liddon, H.P., *St. Paul's First Epistle to Timothy* (Wipf & Stock, 2007), p19.

24. Tidball, Derek & Diane, *The Message of Women* (IVP, 2012), p49.

25. Foner & Branham, *Lift Every Voice* (University of Alabama Press, 1998), p179.

26. Payne, Philip B., *Man and Woman, One in Christ* (Zondervan, 2009), p445.

27. Ibid, p458.

28. Scott, Martin, *For Such a Time as This* (P. S. Promotions, 2000), p146.

29. Boccia, Maria L., *Hidden History of Women Leaders in the Church. Journal of Biblical Equality*. Sept, 1990.

30. Fourth Synod of Carthage. 398 AD.

31. Council of Chalcedon, Canon #15.

32. Ponsonby, Simon, *God is For Us* (Monarch, 2013), p438.

33. Wright, N.T., a paper delivered at St John's College, Durham, on 4th Sept 2004.

34. Bilezikian, Gilbert, *Beyond Sex Roles* (Baker, 1985), p161.

35. Brown, Colin, *NIDNTT* (Zondervan, 2003), Vol 3, p1064.

36. Lawrence O. Richards, *The Word Bible Handbook* (Word Books, 1982), p685.

37. Keener, Craig S., *Paul, Women and Wives* (Hendrickson, 1992), p184.

CHAPTER 9
THE KINGDOM
MAGNA CARTA!

In Galatians 3:28 Paul writes what Paul K. Jewett refers to as the "Magna Carta of Humanity, the great charter of Christian equality between male and female"[1] and Klyne Snodgrass calls "the most socially explosive text in the Bible."[2]

"There is neither Jew nor Gentile, neither slave nor free, neither male nor female, for you are all one in Christ Jesus."

Others have identified this particular text as the "Emancipation Proclamation for Women". Egalitarians believe that Galatians 3:28 contains a revolutionary Christian principle for fundamental human rights. For them, the profound truth of this text is that in Christ, women have been liberated from the slavery and servitude of patriarchy.

Some scholars believe that this was an early baptismal formula for new believers, as it follows on from v27. It is also a supreme and decisive response to the popular prayer which devout Jewish men would pray daily, thanking God that they weren't a woman, a gentile or a slave.

On this passage both Complementarians and Egalitarians agree on the fact that all are equal when it comes to the position of salvation, but differ on the practical implications, which are of huge importance. Let's look at these great statements of equality:

1. "neither Jew nor Gentile"

Paul constantly battled against the hostility between Jew and Gentile. However, his position is clear. Jewish believers could not foist circumcision or Old Testament ceremonial stipulations on Gentile believers. Both are justified by faith. Gentiles would be as free as Jews to function in the Church without restriction. The old has gone and the new order has arrived in Christ.

2. "neither slave nor free"

The Apostle is teaching that now everyone has the chance to be promoted into the family of God with equal status, which at the time was totally counter cultural. Romans were obsessed with status and their clothing reflected it, even down to some wearing thin or thick purple stripes to denote position. Martin Goodman, a leading scholar of the Roman world put it like this:

"On the public level, Roman society was highly stratified on the basis of birth and wealth. The social and political status of each adult male citizen was fixed at irregular censuses … On the domestic scale … the only fully legally recognised persons … in each family unit was its male head, the paterfamilias."[3]

But the division in society was irrelevant in the Church. Writing to Philemon, Paul makes it clear that whether one is a slave-owner or a slave, wealthy or poor, in the Church status is simply "one in Christ"!

In his commentary on Galatians, F.F. Bruce writes, "This could mean for example, that someone who was a slave in the outside world might be entrusted with spiritual leadership in the church, and if the owner of the slave was a member of the same church, he would submit to that spiritual leadership."[4]

Now that is what I call radical!

3. "no male and female"

Paul is a theologian of the new creation and writes *"no male AND female."* The words he uses for "male and female" are quoted from Genesis 1:27, the original creation story in which humanity is seen as a unity with no gender distinction. Paul is clearing the ground of privilege and hierarchy and although recognising differences, states that such count for nothing and are irrelevant in Abraham's family, the Church. As Scot McKnight writes, "The word 'one' evokes God's oneness and God's design for oneness among His created beings. What is Paul claiming here? He is – and notice this carefully – contending that in Christ we return to Eden's unity, equality and oneness."[5]

N.T. Wright, referred to by *TIME* Magazine as "one of the most formidable figures in the world of Christian thought" and by *Newsweek* as "the world's leading New Testament scholar" also suggests that Paul is quoting Genesis 1:27 (*"male and female He created them"*) as part of his argument that males are no longer privileged, thus circumcision is now irrelevant.

It was the Fall that distorted this relationship, but redemption comes through Christ and it is in the Church where the restored mutuality should be exhibited. Sadly, it is often the last place to be seen. Now, says Paul, there is a new city, a new citizenship where everyone counts and has the same status.

Invisible women in the Roman Empire became visible in Christ. In Christ, all ethnicity, class, status and gender differences are transcended. Paul says it like this: *"neither circumcision nor uncircumcision means anything"* but what counts is *"the new creation"*! (Galatians 6:15). In the light of 2 Corinthians 5:17 this is a very significant phrase which some scholars think points towards a possibility that Paul is teaching that this "new creation" actually supersedes Eden. David Harvey, a lecturer at Mattersey Hall refers to Revelation 21 which would seem to imply that God doesn't rewind things when He "renews all", but rather He perfects them.

Before moving on, let me state clearly that transcending differences does not mean eradicating them. People are still male and female, black and white, Jew and Gentile, but in the Kingdom of God it makes no difference.

I recall a conversation I had with Dr John Andrews, Principal of Mattersey Hall, who when referring to this verse, said to his students, "What would you say if you were told 'no black people are able to lead in the church, or no poor people, or no Jews?' People would say that's not on, yet when the Church says, 'no women' can lead in the Church, it somehow becomes acceptable!"

When this is thought through seriously, often the light switches on. When it comes to ministry and leadership in the Church we would not dream of treating a millionaire differently to a beggar, nor a Jew to a Gentile, yet shamefully, two thousand years after Christ's redeeming work on the cross, churches still try to justify the restriction and subordination of women. It has to and must change.

Jackie Pullinger, renowned for her amazing ministry in Hong Kong, was once asked by a highly respected Bible teacher, "Which Bible character do you most identify with?" Without pausing she answered immediately, "David". He was shocked and said he had supposed it would be a woman, like Deborah, for example. She replied, "Why would I answer in terms of gender when you asked about character?!"[6]

This is the heart of this great verse in Galatians. Character not gender is the issue. This milestone verse in the New Testament is at the heart of the Kingdom. Everything is changed as Carolyn James writes in her book *Half the Church*:

"The community of God's people should be the epicentre of human flourishing – where men and women are encouraged and supported in their efforts to develop and use the gifts God has given them wherever He stations them in His world ... God never envisioned a world where His image bearers would do life in low gear or be encouraged to hold back, especially when suffering is rampant, people are lost, and there is so much kingdom work to do."[7]

Similarly, in his commentary on Galatians, F.F. Bruce quoting Galatians 3:28 concludes,

"No more restriction is implied in Paul's equalising of the status of male and female in Christ than in his equalising of the status of Jew and Gentile, or of slave and free person. If in ordinary life existence in Christ is manifested openly in church fellowship, then, if a Gentile may exercise spiritual leadership in church as freely as a Jew, or a slave as freely as a citizen, why not a woman as freely as a man?"[8]

I fully endorse this statement.

4. "for you are all one in Christ Jesus"

In Galatians 3:26 Paul has said, *"For you are all sons of God...".* He is speaking of both men and women and laying a foundation for what is to come in verse 28, which is that all are one in Christ Jesus and status is irrelevant.

Paul says that both male and female are "sons" (or children) of God, so any discrimination against women is a gross distortion of Holy Scripture, which clearly states that there is no difference. Galatians 3:28, *"there is neither ... male or female",* is the clearest reference to the male-female relationship anywhere in Paul's letters, so all other passages relating to this matter must be read through this lens. Galatians was also one of the first New Testament books to be written, years before either Corinthians or Timothy.

It is vital that we don't miss the fact that marriage is not mentioned here. A woman gained status in the Jewish community primarily through marriage to a circumcised male and by bearing sons who would ultimately be circumcised. Not any more says Paul. A woman's role need not be limited to wife and mother; even if she is single she has full equality. Often I cringe when I hear men claiming that a woman can only function in ministry if she has a male covering. Not only is this nonsense, but worse, I believe it dishonours Christ who is *the Head* of the Church.

The truth proclaimed in Galatians 3:28 announces a Kingdom distinct from anything else in this world. A new society, a redemptive movement with a prophetic visual glimpse of Paradise restored, with rich and poor, black and white, Jew and Gentile, men and women, singing the same tune where there is no struggle for superiority or power, but an environment where the Church revels in His love and unites to display to the world God's new order. I like the way J. Lee Grady puts it:

"Paul's words were a sort of Declaration of Independence, a decree of liberation for all who would be excluded from the life of the church by religious-minded Pharisees. This is why some scholars call Galatians 3:28, 'The Magna Carta of Humanity.' In this verse Paul announced that the Church would not be an all-white boys club, controlled by wealthy patriarchal forces. No – God recognises no one by skin colour, economic class or gender. The Holy Spirit's gifts and callings are distributed freely as the Spirit determines (1 Corinthians 12:11)."[9]

Endnotes:

1. Jewett, Paul, K., *Man as Male and Female* (Eerdmans, 1975), p142.

2. Snodgrass, Klyne. *"Galatians 3:28: Conundrum or Solution?"* in *Women, Authority and the Bible* (InterVarsity Press, 1986).

3. Goodman, Martin, *The Roman World 44 BC – AD 180* (Routledge, 2013), p17.

4. Grenzo & Kjesbo, *Women in the Church* (IVP, 1995,) p104.

5. McKnight, Scot, *The Blue Parakeet* (Zondervan, 2008), p166.

6. Forster, Faith & Roger, *Women and the Kingdom* (Push Publishing, 2010), p3.

7. James, Carolyn Custis, *Half the Church* (Zondervan, 2010), p76.

8. Bruce, F.F., *Commentary on Galatians* (Eerdmans, 1982), p190.

9. Grady, J. Lee., *25 Tough Questions about Women and the Church* (Charisma House, 2003), pxii.

CHAPTER 10
DISCRIMINATE
OR LIBERATE?

In Dr Susan Stubbs Hyatt's book, *In the Spirit We're Equal,* she writes about the culture of the times of the King James translators. In fact, King James himself was well known for his low view of women.

"When the monarchy was re-instated in 1660, the throne had the on going task of stabilizing society, and the idea of the divine right of kings remained intact. This doctrine intensified the sense of authority already inherent in the head-of-State/head-of-Church concepts. The English King was now authoritative in the state as 'King', that is, as God's designated ruler of the earthly kingdom, and as 'high priest', that is as God's representative earthly ruler of the Church. Nowhere in Scripture is this taught. Nevertheless, this convenient notion of 'divine order' was extended to the home. According to this teaching, the home was to be seen as a little kingdom where the male was to rule as king of 'his castle' in the same way as the King of England was to rule the State. Furthermore, the home was also to be seen as a little church, where the man was to rule as 'high priest' in the same way that the King was to rule the Church of England. So the man was now 'king and priest' of the home with woman as subject both politically and

155

religiously. This is probably the first time that the link was made between the two separate 'roles' of 'head-of-home' and 'priest-of-the-home', so commonly taught among Pentecostal/Charismatics today. Yet nowhere in the New Testament are these roles taught. And nowhere in the New Testament are they linked. And nowhere in the New Testament is the male given responsibility to dominate the female. It is expedient for us to understand that the formulators of the prevailing, traditional theology about women maintained the pagan ideas that women are evil, inferior, unclean and unequal. It is equally important to realize that Jesus taught, by precept and example, a theology of womanhood that was totally opposite to this."[1]

The constant stereotyping of gender roles has been behind some of the disrespectful accusations in recent times that have blamed current social problems on women not taking their place in the home, as well as evangelicals calling for men to be real men and keep them there. Certain books have been written which have summoned Christian men to be stronger, bolder and more authoritative; to take their rightful place in home and the church. Well, it is clear to me in Scripture that a man's rightful place is in *partnership*, not *headship*. I am ashamed to say that although I have fathered three children, not once did I change a nappy. Now every week in our local church, I see men taking their babies and changing them. Are those men less masculine? I challenge any reader to go and ask them that question! Even in biblical times, the role of raising children was a God-given responsibility of both parents. The distinction between home and work was not like it is today and often both were in close proximity. Women were often involved in the family business, as seen in Proverbs chapter 31.

Faith and Roger Forster in their book *Women and the Kingdom*, point out that contrary to popular belief, the only time in the

Bible when someone is told to obey their marriage partner is when Abraham is told to obey his wife Sarah. See Genesis 21:12 where the word rendered "listen" is disguised by the NIV, but in fact is the same word rendered "obey" that appears in Genesis 22:18. Also mentioned is the fact that the only occasion where Sarah humorously refers to Abraham as "lord" was in regard to them having intercourse when she was 90 years of age in order to receive the promised child![2]

Every Christian has been given "grace" through which they can function and play a vital role in the building up of the body of Christ. Note that the phrases in Ephesians 4:7-13 below, "each of us" and "God's people", include women. There is no distinction here. Church is not a man's world, it's Christ's world, and anyone who seeks to discriminate is on dangerous ground.

"But to each one of us grace has been given as Christ apportioned it … It was he who gave some to be apostles, some to be prophets, some to be evangelists, and some to be pastors and teachers, to prepare God's people for works of service, so that the body of Christ may be built up until we all reach unity in the faith and in the knowledge of the Son of God and become mature, attaining to the whole measure of the fullness of Christ."

A survey in *Christianity Today* magazine stated that in a recent poll, 88% of the respondents said that there was a lot of confusion about the roles of males and females in the Christian world. 78% said, "Christian leaders need to speak on the subject." So over three quarters who responded pleaded for Christian leaders to provide some clear teaching on men and women in the Church. The reality is that many do not speak out because it is easier not to. Too many church leaders are not only walking on eggshells, they are preaching on eggshells. I believe there are many church leaders who, deep down, feel uncomfortable with the patriarchal spirit that has persisted, but find it easier to live with it rather than rock the boat.

I gave a series of talks on this subject and I remember being approached by a lady afterwards who thanked me for what I'd said, but also told me she had never heard this preached on before. She commented that it was too late now for her, as she had been held back all her life, but she was grateful that there was hope for the next generation.

Discriminate or liberate? This is the decision the Church has to take. I hope that something in this book, maybe just the title of this chapter, will provide the strength and courage for leaders to emancipate women and empower the Church. Every church leader will one day give an account for the flock entrusted to them. I don't think the Chief Shepherd expects us under-shepherds to treat His sheep any differently to how He did.

Endnotes:
1. Stubbs Hyatt, Susan, *In the Spirit We're Equal* (Hyatt International Ministries Inc., 1999), pp78-80.
2. Forster, Roger and Faith, *Women and the Kingdom* (Push Publishing, 2010), p13.

CHAPTER 11
A FIVEFOLD CALL
TO THE CHURCH

There is only one reason why I have written this book, which is to appeal to churches to allow everyone, both men and women, full and equal participation in the service of Jesus Christ. My plea is five-fold, which is the focus of this chapter.

1. We must Reconsider the Scriptures

As Christians, when it comes to faith and practice, we must always look to the word of God. Psalm 119:105 says, *"Your word is a lamp to my feet and a light for my path."* I have taken you back to Genesis 1-3 and we have also looked at the role of women in the Old Testament. We have looked at how Jesus treated women in the Gospels and how women operated in the New Testament. We also looked at how Paul dealt with the issue specifically in difficult passages. I have opened up texts that you may not have heard preached on very often. We have dealt with the issues and what we have seen is this: Men and women were created equal, both made in the image of God. One was not made superior, the other was not made inferior.

They were both given identical roles. In society they were told to rule. In the family they had equal roles – to both be fruitful.

Both were responsible for the Fall, so the prejudice, bias and negativity that has been levelled against Eve throughout society over many centuries has been unwarranted and unjustified. I have given many quotes which illustrate some of the hostility against women because of the prejudice against Eve. Tertullian, one of the early Church fathers, is indicative of this kind of prejudice: "You – women are the devil's gateway. You are the unsealer of that forbidden tree. You are the first deserter of that Divine Law. You are she who persuaded him, who the devil was not valiant enough to attack. You destroyed so easily God's imaged man on account of your desert, women that is death, even the Son of God had to die. Women – you take the blame!"[1]

It is this kind of unbiblical teaching that has negatively coloured society over centuries, creating a culture which resulted in male dominance. This was not the will of God, but a consequence of the Fall of both Adam and Eve. A negative attitude towards women has been embedded in cultures around the world by Roman, Jewish and Greek philosophers, but when Christ came, He came to set the captives free. He came to bring freedom to those who were bound. THANK GOD!

The Gospel confronted the world and its treatment of women. Jesus Christ has done more in the world for women than anyone else has ever done. He levelled the playing field. In Acts 2, in the new community, the Holy Spirit *"filled them all"* just as the prophet Joel had prophesied:

"I will pour out my Spirit on ALL people. Your sons and daughters will prophesy, your old men will dream dreams, your young men will see visions. Even on my servants, both men and women, I will pour out my Spirit in those days." (Joel 2:28-29)

In the upper room there was no distinction between gender or class. The New Testament women functioned according to the five-fold gifts in Ephesians. Women functioned in leadership roles. Nowhere in the New Testament are church roles defined on the basis of gender.

Loren Cunningham, in his book *Why Not Women?*, tells a story of Sophie Miller, who went out as a missionary to Columbia in the late 1940s. Sophie worked near where the Orinoco and Amazon rivers come together and started at least 500 churches. Since she had been taught that a woman should keep silent in the church, however, she taught all her converts outside the building! When it rained, she would take all her students under some kind of shelter, so that they didn't get wet. Cunningham says, "Was this necessary? Is the church a building? Of course not, the church is the people."[2]

These are the kind of ridiculous situations that occur through the prejudice against women in church life. May Eleanor Fray, an Assemblies of God Evangelist asks this, "God Almighty is no fool, I say it with reverence, would He fill a woman with the Holy Spirit, endow her with ability, give her a vision of souls, and then tell her to shut her mouth?"[3]

I remind you of the preponderance of scripture. We cannot extinguish the surpassing influence of Scripture because we struggle with a few difficult verses. We must reconsider the Scriptures.

2. We Must Celebrate Our Diversity

Equality does *not* mean sameness. All men are equal, all women are equal, men and women are equal, but they are not the same. It is okay to be different. It is okay to be you. In fact, it is vital that you are you, as it is only by being you, as a man or woman, that you can fulfil the purpose of God for your life.

When it comes to the purpose of God, the same things that are open to men are open to women. Psalm 139 says we are all *"fearfully and wonderfully made."* It says that all the days ordained for us were written in His book before any of them came to be. When you, as a woman or man, entered this world, you came with a plan that God has for your life. You were sent into the world and God's already got a book written about you.

When babies arrive in this world, the first thing that happens when they emerge from their mother is that someone looks at their genitals. From the very moment of birth, then, the cultural stereotyping begins. The colour of our clothing is decided; the nature of our toys is decided. Boys are given adventure and action toys, whilst girls are given gifts that relate to cooking, cleaning and child-rearing! Sadly, the joy of our parents may also be decided. How many times has "it's a boy" or "it's a girl" brought disappointment? Yet we should recognise that all life is a gift from God and each person is unique with a special destiny. Though male and female bodies are different, especially in the area of sexual organs (for the purpose of reproduction) we realise that it is not our body that is made in the image of God, because God does not have a body – He is Spirit.

The image of God confers on us moral power, creative capacity, community, the ability to love and be loved. These qualities are the image of God in humanity. You are more than your body. The Bible describes your body as an earthly tent. It doesn't say an earthly "female" or earthly "male" tent. We are all people, created by God, who live in our temporal bodies. Our destiny and ministry is not to be decided by our earthly tent. It will be interesting in heaven to discover whether there will be male and female tents, since we are told in Scripture that there won't be any marriage there. That thought is another reminder of how foolish it is for us to get so caught up with the temporary.

Galatians 2:6 teaches us that *"God does not judge by external appearance"* and Acts 10:34 that, *"God shows no partiality."* It is okay to be male or female, black or white, Jew or Gentile, English, Asian, African or any other race. Let us celebrate our diversity, remembering that in His Kingdom there are no distinctions. Gilbert Bilezikian says, "Discrimination of any kind is a monstrous denial of oneness of the Church of Christ."[4]

Part of celebrating our diversity means choosing not to judge the circumstances of others, based on how we live our life. It is okay to be different. In some families the woman works and supports the man, who is mainly responsible for raising the children. Why should this not be okay? Nowhere in the Bible does it say that children are the woman's responsibility. The teaching of Scripture is that the responsibility lies with both. I know many men who have been supported through Bible college by their wives. My wife held down three jobs to support me through college, whilst also caring for our first child!

Cultural stereotypes colour our thinking. It's fine for men to cook and iron. Why shouldn't it be? I remember my own mother with *Mrs Beeton's Cookery Book*. Back then it was considered a woman's place to cook and keep house. My mother never learned to drive as it was a "man thing". Today, however, there are more male chefs than female ones. Just because a man is a chef does not make him effeminate!

Maybe in your family, the roles are very traditional. That is fine too. Diversity is allowed. The key in marriage is for the man and woman to agree their roles depending on what works best for them and their family. It does not make a woman masculine or a man feminine if they do things outside the stereotypes that culture dictates.

On careful consideration it would seem that over the centuries we have given more weight and credence to cultural dictates than to God's, but every so often there have been some God-driven people who have broken that mould to live out their God-given destiny. Suzanna Wesley had 19 children, including John and Charles. I reckon just having those two was enough of an achievement, but she was also the wife of a vicar and, in a culture where women were frowned upon, she had a meeting every week where she preached to over 200 people. Often people were turned away because of lack of room. It wasn't the done thing! Can you imagine how many times she was taken to one side and told, "Suzanna you have 19 kids, that is your role in life, that's your ministry"? John Wesley described her as a "preacher of righteousness". Even though he fought against it for many years, eventually he had to accept the fact that God was using his mother to preach.

We must celebrate our diversity. John Ortberg admits to his own struggle in this area with these words:

"In the grace and humour and love of God, I ended up marrying a woman who not only has remarkable gifts of teaching and speaking, she also clearly has stronger leadership gifts than I do. For many years of my life, I was driven by the need to see myself as a leader. For a long chunk of our marriage I could never have perceived that my wife had stronger leadership gifts than I do. Then eventually – reality being such an ugly but persistent little monster – I could perceive it, but only acknowledge it with great pain. And then, eventually, blessedly, came freedom. Freedom to be who God made me to be and to not be who God did not make me to be, and to celebrate and cheer on all that He created in my wife."[5]

3. We Must Confess Our Malpractice

It is never easy to admit you have been wrong, but many times the Christian Church has been wrong and many times the

Church has failed. The history books contain the evidence. At times the Church has lost the truth, smothered the Holy Spirit, and introduced man-made traditions and customs. At times the Church has imposed un-biblical structures. But throughout history, whenever revival has occurred, the Church has repented of its malpractice. Why? Because when revival comes and the Holy Spirit moves, a fresh humility comes, pride is slain and people start to repent, admitting their error. It is revival that has kept the Church alive through the centuries. In fact, whenever the Church was on the verge of dying, God blew with His breath, burned with His fire, poured in His oil and a fresh renewal occurred. The Church was revived, adjusted and got going again. One fact often overlooked is this, every time there has been a revival women have been at the forefront. When the revival has died down, women have been squeezed out.

Throughout history, it has always required someone to "beat a drum" at certain times in order to bring change. Leading up to the Reformation, Friar Johann Tetzel was selling "indulgencies" to people, ripping off the poor, saying that if they paid him money he could get their loved-ones through purgatory faster. It was Luther who had to beat a drum and declare "We are justified by faith alone."

Someone has to beat a drum when there is malpractice, to bring the Church to a place of repentance for its wrong practices. Slavery is one example, mentioned briefly earlier in this book.

Many people know that John Newton, who wrote the song *Amazing Grace*, was saved after a terrible storm in 1748. What a lot of people don't realise is that he didn't stop dealing in the slave trade after his conversion, he carried on. In fact, just afterwards he went to Liverpool, purchased 200 slaves, then travelled across the Atlantic to South Carolina in order to sell them. During the voyage, as 200 men, women and children were shackled together below deck, a third of them dying on the trip, Newton was sitting in the comfort of his cabin studying a Latin Bible! When he arrived in the US and sold on the slaves, he took the money, sat in church and praised God. All told, he carried on dealing in slavery for another decade. Why? Because at that time slavery was not wrong in the eyes of most Christians. It wasn't a problem to anybody, it was just part of their culture.

Newton wrote the words, "I was blind, but now I see." Later, he did see. He received revelation of the evil of slavery, left the trade and became a church minister. It was said of him afterwards that it was impossible to spend half an hour with the man, without him mentioning his terrible, deep regret for all his years spent inflicting this blight on humanity.

In 1839, when the Slavery Abolition Act was passed, all the slaves in the British Empire were released. It was Christians like Wilberforce who fought against slavery that eventually reversed the malpractice!

More recently, in South Africa, the Dutch Reformed Church did something very similar. Historically, the 350-year old institution had strongly taught white supremacy, and argued biblically that Apartheid was the will of God! They believed that:

- South Africa's Apartheid laws were God's will
- Races should be kept apart
- Whites should have better opportunities as they heed God's "favour"
- Mixed marriages and relationships are discouraged so races remained "pure"
- God is the "Great Divider".

There were Christians who fought against this segregation. Two of the most influential were Bishop Desmond Tutu and

Trevor Huddleston. In 1992, the leaders of that denomination made a statement to this effect: "Apartheid was not only wrong, it was sinful and a travesty of the Gospel."[6] They had to admit, "We were wrong."

Whenever we realise that we have been wrong, we need to confess it and change. When things are wrong they must be put right. We must confess our malpractice, otherwise we will not liberate and we will continue to discriminate. Many times our society has had to admit we got it wrong. The Suffragettes fought for 70 years to win women the right to vote and now every Christian nation in the world allows women to vote. Were they right before, not to allow the women to vote? Of course not. It was based on the skewed thinking that women weren't wise enough to know who should govern them. It is amazing what people can argue in favour of when they are convinced about it, even though they are wrong!

Years ago small children spent long hours in Britain's coal mines dragging heavy wagons. Yes, in Britain. Do you know why they did that? Because animals were expensive, but children were expendable! That is how Britain looked upon it back then. We look back with shame and think, "How awful that we considered animals more valuable than children!" What happened to change this awful circumstance? Someone came with a drum. Social reformers like Shaftesbury and others brought in acts to outlaw the accepted norm in order to change society. Before Booth and the Salvation Army got their great campaign of drum beating going, pubs in Britain had what they called "step stools", so that children could reach the bar to order their gin!

It is hard to believe but even the concept of missionary work was opposed by Christians. When William Carey went to his denominational leaders to ask for support and endorsement to set up a missionary society, one of the leaders said to him, "Young man, sit down. When God pleases to convert the heathen, He will do it without consulting you or me."[7] Do you know what Carey did? He went to India anyway, on his own, and thus began the world-wide missionary movement.

When a thing is wrong it has to be confronted! It is with great regret that I have to say women have had a raw deal in the church and a raw deal from the Church. The words of Elizabeth Cady Stanton, an American social activist, abolitionist and leading figure in the early women's rights movement, make me feel ashamed: "The Bible and the Church have been the greatest stumbling block in the way of women's emancipation."[8]

I was once like the slave owner. Now I'm telling people how to set the slaves free. As someone who had lectured on homiletics and hermeneutics, I was guilty of bad interpretation of Scripture. I was guilty of holding people back because of their gender; of only considering men when it came to leadership in the church. Over recent years God has convicted me and dealt with me to bring me to repentance over my sin, my bad attitudes, and my wrong thinking regarding gender.

Over the last 2000 years, to a large degree, Christ has saved women and the Church has bound them. Many godly Christian women have therefore been forced to use their God-given talents outside the Church. We have had successful business women in industry outside the Church. Successful women leaders, outside the Church. Women leaders in education, politics and many diverse areas outside the Church. Yet inside the Church they have been treated like second-class citizens. The heart of God has been grieved. How the Church has treated women has been un-biblical and unrighteous and we sincerely need to repent. I would like to quote Derek and Dianne Tidball's views on this issue:

"Today, Paul is likely to argue that the refusal to permit women to exercise leadership in the church is what brings the gospel into disrepute. If Paul were writing now, he would surely be rebuking members of the church, both men and women, for compromising with the secular and self-obsessed values of our society and doing so by drawing attention to specific things he would not need to explain, for they would be understood as part of our cultural environment. And he would be instructing the church by reference to biblical illustrations, examples and writings. Given all that Paul writes elsewhere by way of positive appreciation about his female co-workers, who obviously were well instructed in the faith, we suspect he would be rejoicing at the many women who exercise their wonderful teaching and leadership gifts in the church for the sake of the gospel and the glory of Christ."[9]

4. We Must Confront Our Thinking

The well quoted Scripture says, *"As a man thinks in his heart, so he is"* (Proverbs 23:7 AV). Without the constant renewing of our minds culture will always try to squeeze us into its mould. Renewing our minds is not a one-time process, but a continuous one, and as much as we don't like to admit it, the power of culture is strongly influential in our lives. Renewing our minds helps us to grow in our understanding.

As followers of Christ we are challenged to bring into captivity every thought that is contrary to the mind of God. My view, your view, our view of gender, has got to be WORD-SHAPED and not WORLD-SHAPED. We have to confront our thinking and I believe that this is a dark, stronghold issue.

In an earlier chapter I mentioned how Loren Cunningham had challenged the pastor of the world's largest church to utilise the women more. Dr Yonggi Cho replied, "I can't. In Asian culture you can't use women." Today, however, that church is around three quarters of a million strong, and of the 60,000 cell group leaders, 55,000 of them are women. How did that happen? By renewed thinking and by not being dictated to by culture.

David Cartledge in his book, *Apostolic Revolution*, writes:

"Church history shows that in every revival period women have been used of God and recognised, but in a short time have been relegated to inconspicuous positions. However, it also shows that their recognition by God and their involvement in actual ministry continually re-occurs, despite the prejudice of males. Invariably, when a fresh move of the Spirit occurs, women either initiate it or are central to its success."[10] Similarly, Charles Finney said, "The church that silences its women is shorn of half its power."[11]

A hundred years ago, Frederick Franson wrote these words:

"It's amazing how one can get such a false idea that not all God's children should use all their powers in all ways to save the lost world. There are, so to speak, many people in the water about to drown. A few men are trying to save them, and that is considered well and good, but look over there, a few women have untied a boat also to be of help in the rescue, and immediately a few men cry out (standing there, looking idly on and therefore having plenty of time to cry out), 'No, no, women must not help, rather let the people drown.'"[12]

In his book, *For Such a Time as This*, Martin Scott says, "The time has come for Pentecostal women in ministry to leave their arena of debate and simply be who they are and do what God has called them to do."[13]

When A.B. Simpson, founder of the Christian and Missionary Alliance, was criticized for his open policy on women, he responded, "Dear brother, let the Lord manage the women, He can do it better than you, and you turn your batteries against the common enemy."[14]

At a Church leader's conference in Seoul, David Yonggi Cho made the following cutting statement, which he addressed to the American pastors present:

"It breaks my heart at what you have done to your women. You hold them back and relegate them to rather insignificant places of ministry instead of setting them free to minister. It is no wonder Christianity is struggling in your country. You go into spiritual battle with one hand tied behind your back."

Dallas Willard in the book, *How I Changed my Mind About Women in Leadership*, writes, "The issue of women in leadership is not a minor or marginal one. It profoundly affects the sense of identity and worth on both sides of the gender line; and, if wrongly grasped, it restricts the resources for blessing, through the Church, upon an appallingly needy world."[15]

Scott McKnight in *The Blue Parakeet*, tells how he and his family were in Buxton having tea in the home of renowned Professor F.F. Bruce. During their time together he asked Bruce what he thought of the ordination of women.

"I don't think the New Testament talks about ordination," he replied.

"What about the silencing passages of Paul on women?" McKnight asked.

"I think Paul would roll over in his grave if he knew we were turning his letters into torah (law)," he responded.

"Wow!" McKnight thought. "So what do you think, then, about women in church ministries?"

Professor Bruce answered, "I'm for whatever God's Spirit grants women gifts to do."[16]

This, I believe, is what the Bible teaches. Everywhere in the

New Testament where leadership is discussed it is on the basis of gift and spiritual character, never gender. The whole debate about women in church ministry is predicated upon un-biblical thinking. This is made clear by Jesus in Matthew 20:23 (NLT): *"You know that the rulers in this world lord it over their people, and officials flaunt their authority over those under them. **But among you, it will be different.**"*

My conviction is this: it is the enemy, not God, who wants to hold women back. I have discovered that it is not only some men who want to restrict women in ministry, but some women do too. Why? Because it challenges the comfort zones they have always known. There will be times when both men and women need their minds renewed, because their thinking is contrary to the word of God.

We must confront our thinking!

5. We Must Champion the New Community

This is my vision for the Church. A glorious Church of anointed men and women, filled with the Holy Spirit, each using their God-given gifts to serve our wonderful risen Saviour. A Church in which each person humbly respects the others, each loving one another, each totally devoted to Christ, each working together with a mission to the world. That is what we must build.

The Church in the New Testament is not a "top-down" organisation, with a hierarchy of top dogs and big bosses, it is a "bottom-up" organisation characterised by equality and servant leadership (see Jesus' words in Mark 10; see also 1 Peter 5). Leadership in the Church must be characterised by respect, honour and submission, by loving care, by a devoted lifestyle and by divine gifting. Not by status, not by position, not by gender. We must champion this reality in the new community.

We have seen glimpses of it in the past. Catherine Booth co-founded The Salvation Army with her husband, William, who drafted the following Orders and Regulations to be observed by The Salvation Army:

"Women shall have the right to an equal share with men in the work of publishing salvation. A woman may hold any position of power and authority within the Army. A woman is not to be kept back from any position of power or influence on account of her sex. Women must be treated as equal with men in all intellectual and social relationships of life."[17]

My prayer is that every church and denomination would hold the same values.

One of the core values of our church in Newtown, Wales, states that, "Leaders serve with humility and not because of ego, status or position … women are allowed to reach their full potential in Christ and are not to be held back simply because of their gender." Our own church dream calls us to champion the new community, the nature of which is egalitarian. Our dream, goal, ethos and philosophy is to have an egalitarian Church which reflects Galatians 3:28: *There is neither Jew nor Greek, slave nor free, male or female for you are all one in Christ Jesus.* The world is, I believe, waiting to see that kind of church, which truly reflects the mutuality and equality of the true Gospel of Jesus Christ.

Churches who champion the new community will face opposition because this is a spiritual stronghold. I agree with Ed Silvoso, the Argentinian Evangelist, who says, "Satan has spent centuries belittling women and weaving a web of lies into a formidable worldwide network of oppression to hold them down. He knows that when women find out who they really are, his kingdom will come to an abrupt end. He cannot afford to have women walking upright. He desperately needs to keep them down."[18]

Because of this, churches who release women in ministry/ leadership will face criticism from other churches and in some cases, as I have been, be accused of compromise and heresy. But it is a drum that I must beat. Jesus was criticised for how He treated women. People criticised the reformers for beating their drums. Every revivalist has been criticised. Social reformers like Wilberforce, Shaftesbury and others were criticised by their peers. Wesley and Whitfield were banned from their pulpits by their church movements, forcing them to preach in the streets. Martin Luther King beat a drum and he got shot for it. To me this is a hill worth dying on. The price is worth paying.

I am moved by the words of Loren Cunningham. "I see every little girl knowing she is valued, knowing she is made in the image of God and knowing she can fulfil all the potential He has put within her. I see the body of Christ recognising leaders whom the Holy Spirit indicates, the ones who He has gifted, anointed and empowered without regard to race, colour or gender, that this generation would be the one who simply asks 'Who is it that God wants to use?'"[19]

May God help us achieve such, because until we arrive at this place, everybody loses. I want to end this chapter by making the following declaration over women and men:

To all the women reading this:
You are not partially redeemed, you are fully redeemed.

I want you to know that you are not afar off; you have been brought near, just as men have, by the blood of Christ.

I want you to know that man is not the priest of your house; you are the royal priesthood yourself. The Bible teaches the priesthood of ALL believers, not just some believers.

I want you to know that you are not just an heir, you are JOINT and EQUAL heirs with Christ and all God's people.

I want you to know that you are not limited by your gender, only by your dreams.

I want you to know that you are not second-class citizens in Church or in God's kingdom. We are all 'sons' of God, both male and female with equal status. God loves women just as much as He loves men.

I want you to know that you are here for a purpose. You are a person of destiny.

I want you to know that in you there are gifts and abilities that are to be used for Christ. Right now I want to release you from negative words and negative influences, from the bias and prejudice that may have come against you.

I want to set you free in the name of Jesus Christ to fulfil every role that God has called you to. There are Apostles like Junia, teachers like Priscilla, prophets like Phillip's daughters, pastors like Nympha at Colossi, evangelists like the woman at the well, leaders like Esther, lovers like Mary, successful business women like Lydia. Whether you are called to be a leader, preacher, follower, teacher, pastor or evangelist, there should be no limits put on you because of your gender. You have not been called to live under the reign of man but Christ, and it is to His Lordship alone that we all bow.

To all the men that are reading this:

I want to say again, there is no ground for distinction. We are living in a lost world. Society is getting increasingly darker and Jesus Christ is coming soon. We do not just need some of God's people to bear light, it needs every one of us. We don't need just some hands to the plough, we need every hand. Hell is against us, but by God's grace if we can build an egalitarian church where everyone is equal and free to serve within their gifting, hell will hate it, but the world will love it.

The Church is the new community – the undivided body of Christ – and we must champion it. As men we need to recognise how poor we would be if women were removed from their crucial roles in our society. Many men rely on women for employment, justice, government, education, wealth creation, medicine, law enforcement, and increasingly the armed forces. Yet in the Church many are side-lined, restricted and prevented from playing a full role in God's new community. The costly result is that many times, roles are assigned to less-gifted males and the Church is robbed of more-gifted females. It makes no sense, but even more so when it is on the basis of the incorrect understanding of a few verses of Scripture. Men, rise up and release and empower women to play their part!

* * *

In closing, I quote from Andrew Walker of Kings College London:

"It used to be thought in the early twentieth century that people who promoted women's leadership in churches – either as preachers or pastors – were liberals, and opponents of women's ministry were conservatives. Such a position in the early twenty first century is untenable; scholarship has unearthed a treasury of women's roles in Bible and history and there really is no excuse for misreading Scripture and ignoring historical evidence in the name of some supposed unmoveable and immutable orthodoxy. While it is certainly the case that there are those who oppose the ministry of women in the church on principled grounds, all too often the root cause is misogyny and there is no room for ambiguity here: hatred of women is sin."[20]

I am proud to belong to the Assemblies of God and honour the incredible work and ministry done by women in this great movement around the world. I think the comments of George Wood, the leader of AOG in the USA, are worth quoting:

"The official position is that there is no position that is off-limits to a woman in credentialed ministry in the Assemblies of God. This has been a historic position. My mother went out as a single minister to northwest China in 1924 when the Assemblies of God was only 10 years of age. We've had not only women missionaries but also women pastors. We've had women evangelists. We've had women scholars, professors — you name it. I'm very unhappy when I hear in our own Fellowship those who don't hold to what is our historic position on women in ministry. The Assemblies of God is a Pentecostal body. We have a very distinct view of the role of women in ministry and the prophecy of Joel that in the last days God would pour out His Spirit upon all flesh. I'm personally very concerned about the incursion into the Pentecostal movement and the Assemblies of God of persons who are not Pentecostal, who bring reformed theology and their view of highly hierarchical structure — whether it's through seminars they've attended, or whatever — and miss utilizing well over half of the workforce that is available to the gospel of Jesus Christ."[21]

Endnotes:

1. Cunningham and Hamilton, *Why Not Women?* (YWAM, 2000), p234.

2. Ibid, p41.

3. Wacker, Grant, *Heaven Below* (Harvard University Press, 2001), p169.

4. Bilezikian, Gilbert, *Beyond Sex Roles* (Baker, 1985), p128.

5. Johnson, Alan F., *How I Changed my Mind About Women in Leadership* (Zondervan, 2010), p182.

6. Sheler, Jeffrey L., *The Era of Collective Repentance*, US News & World Report 119, no1, 1995, pp10-11.

7. Solomon, Robert M., *The Prayer of Jesus* (Armour Publishing, 2009), p130.

8. Deaville, Walter F., [BOOK TITLE] (Moody Press, 1925), p54.

9. Tidball, Derek & Diane, *The Message of Women* (Inter-Varsity Press, 2012), p267.

10. Cartledge, David, *The Apostolic Revolution* (Paraclete Institute, 2000), p317.

11. Tucker, Ruth A., *Women in the Maze* (InterVarsity Press, 1992), p252.

12. Ibid, p179.

13. Scott, Martin, *For Such a Time as This* (P. S. Promotions, 2000), p176.

14. Ruth A. Tucker and Walter Liefeld, *Daughters of the Church* (Zondervan, 1987), pp287-288.

15. Johnson, Alan F., *How I Changed my Mind About Women in Leadership* (Zondervan, 2010), p11.

16. McKnight, Scot, *The Blue Parakeet* (Zondervan, 2008), p207.

17. Galli, Mark, *131 Christians Everyone Should Know* (B&H Publishing, 2010), p299.

18. Grady, J. Lee, *The Truth Sets Women Free* (Charisma House, 2009), p209.

19. Cunningham & Hamilton, *Why Not Women?* (YWAM, 2000), p13.

20. Forster, Faith & Roger, *Women and the Kingdom* (Push Publishing, 2010), p4.

21. Wood, Rev George, *Enrichment Magazine*, Spring 2015, pp59-63.

CHAPTER 12
RELEASING THE
BALL AND CHAIN

Thankfully, more and more churches are recognising the truth regarding women and their public ministry and leadership. The difficulty comes when local church leadership, having received this fresh revelation, wants to implement changes. This will have its challenges, so having been on this journey, for what it is worth, here is my advice.

a. Soak in the Scriptures and be clear on what you see. There is a lot of historical baggage and tradition that does not surrender easily to change. It is not enough to simply start releasing women, you must be sure of the theological foundation for releasing them. We don't use women in spite of Scripture, but because of Scripture.

b. Teach the Scriptures to your current leaders, movers and shakers. This is a subject that cannot be fudged and requires unity and strong conviction. Following arrival at that point, clear teaching should be brought to the whole church. We need more sermons on the powerful and significant ministry of women in the Bible, and of its legitimacy in the Church.

c. Recognise that cultural change takes time and there is always a natural drift back to default mode. This is another reason why strong leadership is essential in church life. Change rarely comes through one sermon. Repetition is what brings about change. Church change rarely comes in one big leap, but in many small steps. Another reason why this issue gets resistance is because, in my opinion, it is an enemy stronghold. Why would the devil want to see two thirds of the church released in their gifting?!

d. Accept the fact that not everyone will agree. Not even all women will agree. Once a church comes to a conviction on this issue, it must be strong and even willing to accept that some people may leave. There are times when a church leadership must name the hill that is worth dying on. Bill Hybels knows this too well. He says, "Many devout, intelligent Christians disagree with our conclusions. There will come a day when we will all find out the degree to which we have veered from God's perfect wisdom, in this issue and many others. Until then, I hold this position, humbly but firmly. I am willing to take the risk of encouraging women to do what I believe Scripture asks of them – to make themselves fully available to the full range of spiritual gifts." He goes on to say "I can't imagine doing senior leadership in a church without the full participation of women at every level."[1]

e. Resist tokenism. Great damage is done when people are chosen just to make things look right. This is not a matter of spiritual window-dressing. If you do not have any gifted women leaders, don't appoint any women. The same applies to men too! Just settle the principle: all appointments to leadership and ministry are on the basis of GIFT, NOT GENDER!

f. Celebrate the gifts of both men and women equally. Model equality. Train people equally. Use single as well as married people (40% of today's Church are single people). Get used to thinking "people" not "men". Keep reminding yourself that if Jesus and the apostles sanctioned women with high capacity roles, so can we.

g. Avoid the nonsense. Renowned Chinese teacher, Watchman Nee, benefitted greatly from the teaching of two Chinese missionaries/leaders. When they visited him one day, he wanted his church to hear them, but there was a problem – they were women and therefore could not teach the men. In order to "fulfil the letter of the law" he strung a curtain along the middle of the meeting room. The two Chinese missionaries taught the ladies on one side of the curtain while the men sat and listened on the other side![2] It's time we owned up to the ridiculous games we play and recognise that we are supposed to be bringing a unique and revolutionary message to the world, not bowing down to a broken and godless system of male domination.

h. Practise true biblical leadership. There is no place in the Church for hierarchical structures of leadership. Leadership is not male. Jesus is Lord and the divine will is that the redeemed Church of God exhibits to the world something the world can never replicate – which is men and women using their God-given gifts without restriction and in mutual submission to each other and the Lord Jesus Christ. That image is a nightmare to the powers of darkness!

i. Resist bad practice. A relatively recent phenomenon, which is not helping the egalitarian message, is the practice of what some call "one flesh ministry".

I refer to pastors and their spouses calling themselves, collectively, "Senior Pastors". Whether the stronger gift is in either the man or the woman, I don't find anywhere in Scripture the spiritual gifts of "Pastor's wife" or "Pastor's husband". There is no evidence that when a man/woman is given a leadership gift, that their spouse gets it too.

Undoubtedly, there are times when both husband and wife are

equipped with ministry and leadership gifts, but where that is not so, great damage can be done when a spouse is honoured with a title for which they do not have the gift.

Often the spouse of a leader will have other gifts, which should be recognised for what they are. There is no shame in a spouse admitting that they are gifted differently to their partner. I have witnessed both men and women struggling to perform ministry for which they are not equipped, simply to keep up with a title they shouldn't be carrying. Let me put it clearly. Whether apostle, prophet, evangelist, pastor, elder, deacon or any other ministry – the spouse must operate in their own ministry and not try to be what their spouse is gifted to be. "One flesh" is about marriage, not ministry.

Without clarity in the Church, we will have confusion in the Church. A good test as to whether both a husband and wife are "Senior Pastors/Leaders" is to ask whether one of them would still remain as senior pastor/leader if the other was suddenly removed. Spiritual gifts are not shared gifts but, *to each **one** the manifestation of the Spirit is given for the common good.*" (1 Corinthians 12:7-8)

j. Simply be wise. Wherever there is talk of men and women working together in leadership the issue is raised about the temptations and possible dangers. It is usually said that it is safer to keep the sexes apart. The idea of mixed-gender ministry or mentoring has caused some church leaders concerns regarding the possibility of unhealthy attraction or sexual impropriety.

Knowing something of Augustine's weakness in this area, safeguards seem prudent but perhaps there is the danger of becoming paranoid too? Possidius, a close friend of Augustine, wrote this about his behaviour: "No woman ever set foot in his house, he never spoke to a woman except in the presence of a third person or outside the parlour, he made no exceptions, not even for his elder sister and his nieces, all three of them nuns."[2]

There is great loss to both men and women when we allow potential dangers to rob us of the undoubted blessings we can receive from each other by working together. Billy Graham and Bill Bright were both mentored by Henrietta Mears. Loren Cunningham was greatly impacted by the teaching of Joy Dawson. Within my own Assemblies of God denomination there are many men who owe much to powerful, godly women leaders.

Of course there will be temptations, but that is not a mandate for us to live at a lower level. The writer to the Hebrews says that Jesus, *"was tempted in all points as we are"* but still worked and travelled with women – even when there was a risk of being misunderstood (see John 4). Jesus did not avoid relationships with women, even with those who had a history of sexual sin. Neither did He avoid being alone with women. He is, as always, our supreme example.

Paul also worked closely and travelled with women, yet avoided scandal. There is no doubt that men and women working closely can generate unhealthy attraction, but the solution is not to forfeit the fruitful power of synergy, but to practice wise habits and accountability. As mature Christians both men and women are called to avoid sin, not each other. God forbid that we should need to resort to something mentioned by Felicity Dale in her book *Black Swan Effect*, who speaks of being in a church planter's conference in Los Angeles when the leader of a particular denomination asserted that pastors "should make sure they hire an old and unattractive woman to be their secretary!"[3]

I am sure that esteemed Bible teacher Dr John Stott would not concur with that, having never married yet having a woman, Frances Whitehead, as his personal secretary for over 50 years, who he described as "my omni-competent and faithful secretary." There was love and friendship without scandal.

The truth is this: male and female leaders *must* work together. There is no option here. They need each other. The Church cannot operate properly until we fully understand that the *"gifts to men"* in Ephesians 4 is gender neutral and that human vulnerability is no excuse for men and women not to work together in God's great redemptive plan. Segregation will rob us of our fullest potential and present to the world a distorted image of the new community.

In closing, I think the words of Gordon Fee are a great summary of my plea through this book:

"It seems a sad commentary on the Church and on its understanding of the Holy Spirit that 'official' leadership and ministry is allowed to come from only one half of the community of faith. The New Testament evidence is that the Holy Spirit is gender inclusive, gifting both men and women, and thus potentially setting the whole body free for all the parts to minister and in various ways to give leadership to the others. Thus my issue in the end is not a feminist agenda—an advocacy of women in ministry. Rather, it is a Spirit agenda, a plea for the releasing of the Spirit from our strictures and structures so that the Church might minister to itself and to the world more effectively."[4]

The Gender Revolution is a glorious biblical truth, which must now become a powerful present reality. It is time for us to hear the sound of chains being broken, of gender discrimination being outlawed. It is time for everyone in the Bride of Christ to share equally the glorious emancipation that was paid for by the blood of Calvary's cross. Let the revolution begin and let the Church shake the world!

Sola Deo Gloria!

Endnotes:

1. Johnson, Alan F., *How I Changed my Mind About Women in Leadership* (Zondervan, 2010), p161.

2. Ranke-Heinemann, Uta, *Eunuchs for the Kingdom of Heaven* (Doubleday, 1990), p22.

3. Dale, Felicity, *The Black Swan Effect* (Kingdom Heart Publishing, 2014), p92.

4. Ronald W. Pierce, Rebecca Merrill Groothuis, Gordon D. Fee (eds), *Discovering Biblical Equality Complementarity Without Hierarchy* (IVP Academic, 2012), p254.

RECOMMENDED READING

Alei, Dee, *From Bondage to Blessing: The Redemption, Restoration, and Release of God's Women*, Sovereign World, 2002.

Bailey, Kenneth, E., *Jesus Through Middle Eastern Eyes – Cultural Studies in the Gospels*, SPCK Publishing, 2008.

Beck, James, R, & Gundry, Stanley, N., *Two Views on Women in Ministry*, Zondervan, 2005.

Belleville, Linda, L., *Women Leaders & the Church: Three Crucial Questions*, Baker Publishing Group, 2000.

Bessey, Sarah, *Jesus Feminist: An Invitation to Revisit the Bible's View of Woman*, Howard Books, 2013.

Bilezekien, Gilbert, Beyond Sex Roles: *What the Bible Says About a Woman's Place in Church & Family*, Baker Publishing Group, 1985.

Bruce, Frederick, F., *The Epistles to the Galatians*, Eerdmans

Publishing Group, 1982.

Bristow, John, T., *What Paul Really Said About Women*, Harper & Row, 1988.

Cartledge, David, *The Apostolic Revolution: The Restoration of Apostles and Prophets in the Assemblies of God in Australia*, Paraclete Institute, 2000.

Connell, Karen, *Women in Ministry: A Biblical and Historical Perspective*, CreateSpace, 2013.

Cunningham L & Hamilton D., *Why Not Women?* YWAM Publications, 2000.

Dale, Felicity, *The Black Swan Effect: A Response to Gender Hierarchy in the Church*, Kingdom Heart Publishing, 2014.

Evans, Mary, J., *Woman in the Bible*, Inter-Varsity Press, 1983.

Forster, Faith & Roger, *Women and the Kingdom*, PUSH Publishing, 2010.

Grady, J. Lee, *25 Tough Questions about Women and the Church*. Charisma House, 2003.

Grenz, Stanley, J. & Kjesbo, Denise, M., *Women in the Church*, Inter-Varsity Press, 1995.

Groothius, Rebecca, M. & Pierce, Ronald, W., *Discovering Biblical Equality*, Inter-Varsity Press, 2005.

Groothius, Rebecca, M., *Good News for Women: A Biblical Picture of Gender Equality*, Baker Books, 1997.

Guinness, Michelle, *Woman – The Full Story*, Zondervan, 2003.

Hull, Gretchen, G., *Equal to Serve*, Fleming H. Revell, 1991.

Johnson, Alan F., *How I Changed my Mind About Women in Leadership*, Zondervan, 2010.

Keener, Craig, S., *Paul, Women & Wives*, Hendrickson Publishers, 1992.

Kroeger, Richard, C. & Kroeger, Catherine, C., *I Suffer Not a Woman*, Baker Academic, 1988.

Martin, Faith, *Call Me Blessed*, Eerdmans, 1988.

McKnight, Scot, *The Blue Parakeet: Rethinking How You Read the Bible*, Zondervan, 2010.

Parales, Heidi, B., *Hidden Voices: Biblical Women and Our Christian Heritage*, Smyth & Helwys Publications, 1998.

Payne, Dr Philip, *Man & Woman, One in Christ: An Exegetical and Theological Study of Paul's Letters*, Zondervan, 2009.

Staton, Knofel, *The Biblical Liberation of Women for Leadership in the Church*, Wipf & Stock Publishers, 2003.

Strickland, Danielle, *The Liberating Truth: How Jesus Empowers*

Women, Monarch Books, 2011.

Swidler, Leonard, J., *Biblical Affirmations of Woman*, Westminster John Knox Press, 1979.

Tidball, Derek & Tidball, Dianne, *The Message of Women*, Inter-Varsity Press, 2012.

Torjesen, Karen, J., *When Women were Priests*, HarperCollins, 1995.

Vallotton, Kris, *Fashioned to Reign: Empowering Women to Fulfill Their Divine Destiny*, Chosen Books, 2013.

Ward, Rosie, *Growing Women Leaders*, Bible Reading Fellowship, 2008.

Webb, William, J., *Slaves, Women & Homosexuals: Exploring Hermeneutics of Cultural Analysis*, Inter-Varsity Press, 2001.

Williams, David, *Junia: A Woman, An Apostle*, CreateSpace, 2014.

Wilshire, Leland, E., *Insight into Two Biblical Passages*, University Press of America, 2010.

Wright, N,T., *The Biblical Basis for Women's Service in the Church*, Priscilla Papers, 2006.

Wright, N,T., *Surprised by Scripture*, Harper Collins, 2014.

Zens, Jon, H., *What's With Paul & Women?* Quoir, 2010.

ABOUT THE AUTHOR

Alan L. Hewitt is a Rolls Royce qualified aeronautical engineer who left the industry in 1970 following a call to full-time ministry. After two years in Bible College he pastored a church in Manchester for 13 years, after which he moved to Newtown in Mid-Wales where he has led Hope Church for over 30 years. He currently serves on the Assemblies of God National Leadership Team (GB) and is Area Leader for Wales. Alan is married to Jennifer and they have three children and three grandchildren.